ESSENTIAL BIBLIOGRAPHY OF AMERICAN FICTION

MODERN WOMEN WRITERS

Matthew J. Bruccoli and
Judith S. Baughman,
Series Editors

Foreword by Mary Ann Wimsatt

Facts On File®

AN INFOBASE HOLDINGS COMPANY

MODERN WOMEN WRITERS

Facts On File, Inc.
460 Park Avenue South
New York NY 10016

Library of Congress Cataloging-in-Publication Data

Modern women writers / Matthew J. Bruccoli and Judith S. Baughman, editors;
    foreword by Mary Ann Wimsatt.
    p. cm.—(Essential bibliography of American fiction)
Includes bibliographical references and index.
ISBN 0-8160-3000-6.—ISBN 0-8160-3001-4 (pbk.)
1. American fiction—Women authors—History and criticism—Bibliography. 2. Women and literature—United States—Bibliography. 3. American fiction—Women authors—Bibliography. I. Bruccoli, Matthew J., 1931- . II. Baughman, Judith. III. Series.
Z1231.F4M65 1993
[PS374.W6]
016.813'5099287—dc20   93-8642

A British CIP catalogue record for this book is available from the British Library.

Facts On File books are available at special discounts when purchased in bulk quantities for businesses, associations, institutions or sales promotions. Please call our Special Sales Department in New York at 212/683-2244 or 800/322-8755.

Text design by Catherine Hyman
Cover design by Heidi Haeuser
Composition by Grace M. Ferrara/Facts On File, Inc.
Manufactured by the Maple-Vail Book Manufacturing Group

Printed in the United States of America

10 9 8 7 6 5 4 3 2 1

This book is printed on acid-free paper.

CONTENTS

SERIES INTRODUCTION

These volumes in the *Essential Bibliography of American Fiction* series are largely adapted from author entries in *Facts On File Bibliography of American Fiction, 1919–1988* (1991) and *Facts On File Bibliography of American Fiction, 1866–1918* (1993), known as *BAF*. The *Essential Bibliography of American Fiction* makes *BAF* material on certain widely read and widely studied authors available in a more affordable format. Whereas *BAF* is intended for colleges and university research libraries, the *Essential Bibliography of American Fiction* volumes are revised for high schools, community colleges, and general libraries—as well as for classroom use.

None of the author entries in this new series is a direct reprint from *BAF*. Each entry has been updated to the end of 1992. The primary bibliographies are complete, but the secondary bibliographies have been trimmed. The *Essential Bibliography of American Fiction* entries are modified for general usability by a cross-section of students, teachers, and serious readers. Asterisks now identify the most generally available and most influential secondary books and articles. The asterisks do not designate the best works—which is a matter for argument; the asterisks mark what can be described as "standard" biographical and critical works.

To enhance the usefulness of the *Essential Bibliography of American Fiction* new entries have been compiled for authors who are not in *BAF*—notably writers born after 1940.

The authors in each *Essential Bibliography of American Fiction* volume are eminent fiction writers who have been grouped on the basis of their backgrounds and materials. The selection of the figures was made in consultation with teachers and librarians. Since a writer will appear in only one volume, it was necessary to decide in which of several possible volumes a figure should be placed: Toni Morrison, for example, was assigned to *Modern African American Writers* rather than to *Modern Women Writers*.

Mark Twain declared that ". . . almost the most prodigious asset of a country, and perhaps its most precious possession, is its native literary product—when that product is free and noble and enduring." The power of literature requires collaboration between authors and their readers. The *Essential Bibliography of American Fiction* series endeavors to promote that collaboration.

FOREWORD

This volume makes available essential bibliographical information for the study of ten major American women writers: Willa Cather, Kate Chopin, Carson McCullers, Joyce Carol Oates, Flannery O'Connor, Katherine Anne Porter, Gertrude Stein, Anne Tyler, Eudora Welty, and Edith Wharton. Of these writers, only Chopin (1851–1904), whose explicit feminist concerns in *The Awakening* (1899) and other fiction make her the precursor of late twentieth-century feminism, is identified with the nineteenth century. Among the other authors, Wharton, Cather, and Stein were influenced by the early twentieth century, World War I, and the postwar period. They are also linked by their similar reactions to the circumscribed situation of the woman writer in America, a situation with which they dealt by forsaking their native regions, temporarily or permanently, for places like New York or Europe that afforded expanded social and literary horizons along with the chance to associate with other writers. And of course the reputation of each has profited, as have the reputations of other authors in the volume, from the rapidly growing late twentieth-century interest in the subjects and methods of women authors and the contribution such authors have made to modernism and other literary movements.

As for the other writers represented here, McCullers, O'Connor, Welty, and Porter are the leading women authors of the Southern Renascence, the period stretching from the late 1920s to the end of World War II that saw a remarkable flowering of literary talent in the writing of Ellen Glasgow, William Faulkner, Thomas Wolfe, Richard Wright, Robert Penn Warren, and other prominent twentieth-century figures. Representing recent, contemporary, or postmodern writing are Anne Tyler and Joyce Carol Oates, who depict contemporary urban domestic and social life in colorful, sometimes violent, and innovative fashion—as in Oates's projected cycle of experimental novels viewing America by means of its favorite fictional genres: the family saga and memoir, the Gothic romance, the detective-mystery novel, and the horror novel.

In terms of cultural and literary history the stretch from Kate Chopin to Tyler and Oates is a long one, covering nearly ninety years of a century that has seen unprecedented economic, social, political, and military upheaval. In varying degrees, the authors represented in this volume have been the victims, the beneficiaries, and sometimes the leaders of the new movements in literature developed to portray that upheaval. Chopin, who as artist and social thinker was well in advance of her time, paid a tragically high price for her depiction in *The Awakening* of Edna Pontellier's social, artistic, and sexual liberation. The enraged public outcry against the ideas the novel advanced—that women be granted the same social and sexual independence as men—effectively ended Chopin's literary career. But the topics she broached have been taken up, explored, and inflected in various ways by Cather in *O Pioneers!* and *My Ántonia;* by Edith Wharton in *The House of Mirth, Ethan Frome,* and *The Age of Innocence;* by Eudora Welty in *Delta Wedding* and *The Golden Apples;* by Katherine Anne Porter in *Old Mortality* and the tales in "The Old Order" sequence; and by Oates in *Do With Me What You Will, Solstice,* and *Marya: A Life.* Several of these writers experienced in their lives the social and artistic liberation examined in their works. Cather left her Nebraska home for New York City, where she worked for *Harper's* and *McClure's* magazines while beginning her distinguished series of novels and tales about Nebraska and the American Southwest, an endeavor that eventually took her back to Nebraska. Stein left America early in the century for Europe, where she lived and wrote until her death in 1946, meanwhile guiding and encouraging the work of such other expatriate Americans as Ernest Hemingway and the composer Virgil Thomson. Wharton also left America for Europe, where she became a friend and professional associate of Henry James while developing her own distinctive voice and vision. For McCullers, Porter, Welty, and O'Connor, the Bread Loaf School near Middlebury, Vermont, or the Yaddo artists' colony in Saratoga Springs, New York, provided similar kinds of freedom as well as opportunities for contact with other writers. Moreover, Welty like Cather had worked in New York before and, like Cather, returned to her native region to produce varied, penetrating, and highly imaginative fiction about it. Flannery O'Connor studied in the Writers' Workshop at the University of Iowa, worked at Yaddo where she began her first novel, *Wise Blood,* and then lived in Connecticut until a serious medical condition, disseminated lupus, forced her to return to her native Georgia, the setting of much of her writing.

Among the qualities identifying literature by women as a field distinctive from that by men are an angle of vision expressed through characterization, episode, scene, and authorial commentary that is often compassionate and understanding but as often detached and objective—the latter aspect mirroring, perhaps, the "insider-outsider" status of the woman author in regard to American life and writing; a subtle, carefully crafted examination of the nuances of family and personal relationships; a preoccupation amounting almost to an obsession with precise, vivid detail; and an emphasis, which increases as the century unfolds, on women's lives, women's stories, women's concerns, and the multiple difficulties that women experience, ranging from domestic misery to severe physical abuse. The subject of much women's fiction is not so much the public arena or the quest-and-initiation experience of male characters drawn by Melville or Hemingway as the confrontation of familiar territory and the wringing from it enough substance to make life—whether the actual life lived or the fictional lives depicted—exciting and meaningful.

Paradoxically, some of the writers who proclaim themselves unconcerned with gender are in fact the ones who put it at the heart of especially troubling novels. Oates, for example—born in 1938 and publishing her first book in 1963—did not initially feel connected to the feminist movement. But although she publicly berated university feminists at a conference in 1973, she produced in the same year the novel *Do With Me What You Will,* about a lovely young woman trying to define herself according to masculine codes and rules. In this and other novels such as *Marya,* she portrays young women attracted to or mercilessly victimized by men holding traditional views of women as sexual objects created to serve masculine needs. Similarly, Tyler—who claims she does not feel that gender issues are central to her writing—nevertheless portrays, in such novels as *Earthly Possessions* and *Celestial Navigation,* how a narrow conception of women's role and mission has harmed certain of her fictive women and their families. Tyler, moreover—married and the mother of three children—has been forced steadily, even fiercely, to protect her writing time: she grants interviews only through correspondence and refuses to give lectures or public readings.

The strength of women's literature as a field is demonstrated by the excellent and important women authors who are not included here because of space restrictions. A promising area for further reading and research is provided by the work of Ellen Glasgow, Djuna Barnes, Mary Lee Settle, and Bobbie Ann Mason—in addition to many African-American women writers, some of whom are represented in another volume in this series.

—*Mary Ann Wimsatt*
McClintock Professor of Southern Letters
University of South Carolina

With especial thanks to Peggy Whitman Prenshaw, Judith Giblin James, and Amy Hudock for information and assistance.

USING THE ESSENTIAL BIBLIOGRAPHY OF AMERICAN FICTION

The only basis for the full understanding and proper judgment of any author is what the writer wrote. In order to grasp the significance and value of a literary career, it is necessary to have a sense of the author's body of work. Bibliographies—lists of what the author wrote and what has been published about the author and the author's work—are the crucial tools of literary study.

The reader should always begin with the *primary* bibliography (the list of books *by* the author). What the author wrote is always much more important than what has been written about the works. Everything comes from the works themselves. Great fiction is much more than plot or story. The capacity of literature to move, excite, or gratify the reader results from the writing itself. Every great writer writes like no one else.

Yet writings about a work of literature may enlarge the reader's understanding. There is a point in the study of literature when the reader—in or out of the classroom—needs the help provided by sound, usable scholarship. Criticism varies greatly in its sense and utility. The best critics act as trustworthy intermediaries between the work and the reader, but the reader has the right to reject unhelpful critical material.

After reading the story or novel, the researcher should first consult a comprehensive bibliography of writings about the author's life and work—as cited in the *Essential Bibliography of American Fiction (EBAF)*. An annotated secondary bibliography will provide brief indications of the content of articles and books. Thus a student seeking sources for a critical analysis of Katherine Anne Porter's story "The Jilting of Granny Weatherall" should consult Hilt and Alvarez's *Katherine Anne Porter: An Annotated Bibliography,* which describes twelve articles between 1962 and 1986 that specifically deal with this story. By checking promising *EBAF* Porter articles against Hilt and Alvarez's annotations for these articles, the researcher should be able to identify the most interesting or useful of these secondary materials. And since book-length studies of Porter's work may also offer meaningful treatments of "The Jilting of Granny Weatherall," the student researcher is advised to examine these books. The most accessible and influential book-length studies are marked in *EBAF* by asterisks; almost all of these books have indexes, which will help students easily locate discussions of Porter's story.

Literary biography is not a substitute for the works; but biography augments the understanding of individual works and their function in the author's total achievement. Dr. Samuel Johnson, the great eighteenth-century literary biographer, observed that just as a soldier's life proceeds from battle to battle, so does a writer's life proceed from book to book. The more the reader knows about the writer, the more fully the reader will recognize the material for the fictions.

The author entries in *EBAF* provide guides for extended study of each writer's life and work; that is, they function as tutors for lifetime reading. Knowledge propagates knowledge. All literary activity is a process of discovery. In literary study it is crucial that students connect what they are reading with what they have previously read. Willing readers and students have been impeded by the inability to find out what to read next—or where to look for the answers to their questions. Reference books are portable universities. The *Essential Bibliography of American Fiction* provides keys to reference tools for the writers who secured the genius of American fiction.

PLAN OF THE ENTRIES

All authors selected for the *Essential Bibliography of American Fiction* receive the same treatment. No attempt has been made to indicate the stature of an author by the form of the entry. The length and scope of each entry is determined by the author's career.

The brief headnotes on the entries place the authors in terms of their reputations in their own time and now.

The first section of each author entry is reserved for BIBLIOGRAPHIES. Author bibliographies are traditionally divided into *primary works* (by the author) and *secondary works* (about the author).

The PRIMARY MATERIAL list in each entry begins with all BOOKS written by the subject author, as well as books for which the author had a major responsibility (as a collaborator or a ghost-writer). The next primary section includes LETTERS, DIARIES, NOTEBOOKS and is usually restricted to book-length works. The third primary section, OTHER, includes volumes in which the subject author was involved as contributor, editor, or translator; this list is selective. The final primary section, EDITIONS & COLLECTIONS, includes standard one-volume gatherings and multi-volume editions.

The MANUSCRIPTS & ARCHIVES section identifies the principal holdings of the author's manuscripts, typescripts, letters, and private papers in libraries or other institutional repositories.

A CONCORDANCE is an index of the words in a work or works by an author. Concordances are irreplaceable tools for the study of style and imagery.

The BIOGRAPHIES section is divided into three parts: *Books, Book Sections,* and *Articles* that focus on the author's career rather than on assessments of his or her work. This section is usually followed by INTERVIEWS, which includes book-length collections of interviews and single interviews of special interest.

The section of CRITICAL STUDIES is divided into five parts:

1. *Critical Books;*
2. Book-length *Collections of Essays* by various critics on the author or a single work by the author;
3. *Special Journals* devoted to an author (*Hemingway Review, Flannery O'Connor Bulletin*), as well as single issues of general scholarly journals (*Modern Fiction Studies*) dealing with that author;
4. *Book Sections* of volumes that treat several authors;
5. Journal or newspaper *Articles* that are critical rather than biographical.

In selecting articles, the contributors and editors have kept the resources and requirements of smaller libraries in mind. However, the most influential articles are always included.

TABLE OF ABBREVIATIONS

& c = and other cities
ed = editor or edited by
et al = and others
nd = no date provided
no = number
nos = numbers
Npl = no place of publication provided in the work
npub = no publisher provided in the work
ns = new series
P = Press
passim = throughout the volume
pp = pages
Repub = republished
Rev = revised
Rpt = reprinted
Sect = Section
U = University
U P = University Press
Vol = Volume

The following acronyms are the actual titles of journals:

CLIO
ELH
MELUS
PMLA

WILLA CATHER

Back Creek Valley, Va, 7 Dec 1873–New York City, NY, 24 Apr 1947

Although Willa Cather was recognized during her lifetime as a major literary figure, her novels were attacked as politically irrelevant by leftist critics during the 1930s. Since her death, attention to her work has increased as critics have identified a wealth of myth, allusion, and symbolism in her fiction. The flourishing of the feminist movement in literature has brought renewed interest in Cather's complex women characters. Her fiction is identified with the Midwest farming frontier as portrayed in *O Pioneers!* and *My Ántonia;* but Cather's material also encompassed the Southwest, French Canada, and Virginia.

Bibliographies

*Arnold, Marilyn. *WC: A Reference Guide.* Boston: Hall, 1986. Secondary.
*Crane, Joan. *WC: A Bibliography,* foreword by Frederick B Adams. Lincoln: U Nebraska P, 1982. Primary.

Books

April Twilights. Boston: Badger, 1903. Augmented as *April Twilights and Other Poems.* NY: Knopf, 1923.
The Troll Garden. NY: McClure, Phillips, 1905. Stories.
The Life of Mary Baker G. Eddy and the History of Christian Science by Georgine Milmine. NY: Doubleday, Page, 1909. Ghost-written by WC.
Alexander's Bridge. Boston & NY: Houghton Mifflin, 1912; London: Constable / Boston & NY: Houghton Mifflin, 1912; *Alexander's Bridges.* London: Heinemann, 1912. Novel.
O Pioneers! Boston & NY: Houghton Mifflin, 1913. Novel.
My Autobiography by S S McClure. NY: Stokes, 1914. Ghost-written by WC.
The Song of the Lark. Boston & NY: Houghton Mifflin, 1915. Novel.

My Ántonia. Boston & NY: Houghton Mifflin, 1918. Novel.

Youth and the Bright Medusa. NY: Knopf, 1920. Stories

One of Ours. NY: Knopf, 1922. Novel.

A Lost Lady. NY: Knopf, 1923. Novel.

The Professor's House. NY: Knopf, 1925. Novel.

My Mortal Enemy. NY: Knopf, 1926. Novel.

Death Comes for the Archbishop. NY: Knopf, 1927. Novel.

Shadows on the Rock. NY: Knopf, 1931. Novel.

Obscure Destinies. NY: Knopf, 1932. Stories.

Lucy Gayheart. NY: Knopf, 1935. Novel.

Not Under Forty. NY: Knopf, 1936. Essays.

Sapphira and the Slave Girl. NY: Knopf, 1940. Novel.

The Old Beauty and Others. NY: Knopf, 1948. Stories.

On Writing, foreword by Stephen Tennant. NY: Knopf, 1949. Essays.

Writings From WC's Campus Years, ed James R Shively. Lincoln: U Nebraska P, 1950. Miscellany.

Five Stories, with essay by George N Kates. NY: Vintage/Random House, 1956.

WC in Europe, ed with intro & notes by Kates. NY: Knopf, 1956. Travel letters.

Early Stories of WC, ed with commentary by Mildred R Bennett. NY: Dodd, Mead, 1957.

WC's Collected Short Fiction, 1892–1912, intro by Bennett. Lincoln: U Nebraska P, 1965.

The Kingdom of Art: WC's First Principles and Critical Statements, 1893–1896, ed with commentary by Bernice Slote. Lincoln: U Nebraska P, 1966. Essays & journalism.

The World and the Parish: WC's Articles and Reviews, 1893–1902, 2 vols, ed William M Curtin. Lincoln: U Nebraska P, 1970.

Uncle Valentine and Other Stories: WC's Uncollected Short Fiction, 1915–1929, ed Slote. Lincoln: U Nebraska P, 1973.

WC in Person: Interviews, Speeches, and Letters, ed L Brent Bohlke. Lincoln & London: U Nebraska P, 1986.

Other

The Best Stories of Sarah Orne Jewett, 2 vols, selected & arranged with preface by WC. Boston & NY: Houghton Mifflin, 1925.

Editions & Collections

The Novels and Stories of WC, 13 vols. Boston: Houghton Mifflin, 1937–1941.

The Troll Garden, ed with intro by James Woodress. Lincoln: U Nebraska P, 1983.

WC: *Early Novels and Stories,* ed Sharon O'Brien. NY: Library of America, 1987.

WC: *Later Novels,* ed O'Brien. NY: Library of America, 1990.

Manuscripts & Archives

The major collections are at the Willa Cather Pioneer Memorial, Red Cloud, Nebr; Nebraska Historical Society, Lincoln; the Newberry Library, Chicago; U of Virginia Library; U of Vermont Library; the Houghton Library, Harvard U; the Beinecke Library, Yale U; & the Huntington Library, San Marino, Calif.

Biographies

BOOKS

Ambrose, Jamie. WC: *Writing at the Frontier.* Oxford, UK: Berg, 1988.

Bennett, Mildred R. *The World of WC.* NY: Dodd, Mead, 1951.

*Brown, E K. WC: *A Critical Biography,* completed by Leon Edel. NY: Knopf, 1953.

Brown, Marion Marsh & Ruth Crone. WC: *The Woman and Her Works.* NY: Scribners, 1970.

Brown & Crone. *Only One Point of the Compass: WC in the Northeast.* Danbury, Conn: Archer, 1980.

Byrne, Kathleen D & Richard C Snyder. *Chrysalis: WC in Pittsburgh, 1896–1906.* Pittsburgh: Historical Society of Western Pennsylvania, 1980.

Lewis, Edith. *WC Living: A Personal Record.* NY: Knopf, 1953.

*O'Brien, Sharon. WC: *The Emerging Voice.* NY: Oxford U P, 1987.

Robinson, Phyllis C. *Willa: The Life of WC.* Garden City, NY: Doubleday, 1983.

Sergeant, Elizabeth Shepley. WC: *A Memoir.* Philadelphia: Lippincott, 1953.

WC: A Biographical Sketch, an English Opinion, and an Abridged Bibliography. NY: Knopf, 1927. Probably by WC.

WC: A Pictorial Memoir, photographs by Lucia Woods et al; text by Bernice Slote. Lincoln: U Nebraska P, 1973.

Woodress, James. *WC: Her Life and Art.* NY: Pegasus, 1970.

*Woodress. *WC: A Literary Life.* Lincoln: U Nebraska P, 1987.

BOOK SECTIONS

Butcher, Fanny. "WC." *Many Lives—One Love* (NY: Harper & Row, 1972), 354–368.

Slote, Bernice. "Writer in Nebraska." *The Kingdom of Art,* 3–29.

Vermorcken, Elizabeth Moorhead. *These Two Were Here: Louise Home and WC* (Pittsburgh Pa: U Pittsburgh P, 1950), 45–62.

ARTICLES

Benson, Peter. "WC at *Home Monthly.*" *Biography,* 4 (Summer 1981), 227–248.

Fisher, Dorothy Canfield, "Daughters of the Frontier." *New York Herald Tribune Books* (28 May 1933), 7, 9.

Critical Studies

BOOKS

Arnold, Marilyn. *WC's Short Fiction.* Athens: Ohio U P, 1984.

Bloom, Edward A & Lillian D. *WC's Gift of Sympathy.* Carbondale: Southern Illinois U P, 1962.

Callender, Marilyn Berg. *WC and the Fairy Tale.* Ann Arbor, Mich: UMI, 1989.

Daiches, David. *WC: A Critical Introduction.* Ithaca, NY: Cornell U P, 1951.

Edel, Leon. *WC: The Paradox of Success.* Washington: Reference Department, Library of Congress, 1960.

Fryer, Judith. *Felicitous Space: The Imaginative Structures of Edith Wharton and WC.* Chapel Hill: U North Carolina P, 1986.

*Gerber, Philip L. *WC.* Boston: Twayne, 1975.

Giannone, Richard. *Music in WC's Fiction*. Lincoln: U Nebraska P, 1968.

*Lee, Hermione. *WC: A Life Saved Up*. London: Virago, 1989.

McFarland, Dorothy Tuck. *WC*. NY: Ungar, 1972.

Middleton, Jo Ann. *WC's Modernism: A Study of Style and Technique*. Rutherford, NJ: Fairleigh Dickinson U P, 1990.

Murphy, John J. *My Ántonia: The Road Home*. Boston: Twayne, 1989.

Nelson, Robert J. *WC and France: In Search of the Lost Language*. Urbana: U Illinois P, 1988.

Pers, Mona. *WC's Children*. Uppsala, Sweden: Uppsala U, 1975.

Randall, John H, III. *The Landscape and the Looking Glass: WC's Search for Value*. Boston: Houghton Mifflin, 1960.

Rapin, René. *WC*. NY: McBride, 1930.

*Rosowski, Susan J. *The Voyage Perilous: WC's Romanticism*. Lincoln: U Nebraska P, 1986.

Ryder, Mary Ruth. *WC and Classical Myth: The Search for a New Parnassus*. Lewiston, NY: Mellen, 1990.

Shaw, Patrick W. *WC and the Art of Conflict: Re-Visioning Her Creative Imagination*. Troy, NY: Whitston, 1992.

Skaggs, Merrill Maguire. *After the World Broke in Two: The Later Novels of WC*. Charlottesville: U P Virginia, 1990.

*Stouck, David. *WC's Imagination*. Lincoln: U Nebraska P, 1975.

Thomas, Susie. *WC*. London: Macmillan, 1990.

*Van Ghent, Dorothy. *WC*. Minneapolis: U Minnesota P, 1964.

*Wasserman, Loretta. *WC: A Study of the Short Fiction*. Boston: Twayne, 1991.

Welsch, Roger L & Linda K. *C's Kitchens: Foodways in Literature and Life*. Lincoln: U Nebraska P, 1987.

COLLECTIONS OF ESSAYS

Bloom, Harold, ed. *Modern Critical Views: WC*. NY: Chelsea House, 1985.

Bloom, ed. *Modern Critical Interpretations: WC's My Ántonia*. NY: Chelsea House, 1987.

Murphy, John J, ed. *Five Essays on WC: The Merrimack Symposium*. North Andover, Mass: Merrimack C, 1974.

Murphy, ed. *Critical Essays on WC*. Boston: Hall, 1984.

Murphy & Linda Hunter Adams & Paul Rawlins, eds. *WC: Family, Community, and History*. Provo, Utah: Brigham Young U, 1990.

Rosowski, Susan J, ed. *Approaches to Teaching C's My Ántonia.* NY: MLA, 1989.

Rosowski, ed. *Cather Studies I.* Lincoln: U Nebraska P, 1990.

Schroeter, James, ed. *WC and Her Critics.* Ithaca, NY: Cornell U P, 1967.

Slote, Bernice & Virginia Faulkner, eds. *The Art of WC.* Lincoln: Department of English, U Nebraska, 1974.

SPECIAL JOURNALS

Colby Library Quarterly, 8 (Jun 1968). WC issue.

Colby Library Quarterly, 10 (Sep 1973). WC issue.

Great Plains Quarterly, 2 (Fall 1982). WC issue.

Great Plains Quarterly, 4 (Fall 1984). WC issue.

Legacy, 9, no 1 (1992). WC issue.

Literature and Belief, 8 (1988). WC issue.

Modern Fiction Studies, 36 (Spring 1990). WC issue.

Western American Literature, 7 (Spring 1972). WC issue.

Willa Cather Pioneer Memorial Newsletter (quarterly, 1957–).

Women's Studies, 11, no 3 (1984). WC issue.

BOOK SECTIONS

Auchincloss, Louis. "WC." *Pioneers & Caretakers: A Study of 9 American Women Novelists* (Minneapolis: U Minnesota P, 1965), 92–122.

Beer, Thomas. "Miss C." *The Borzoi 1925* (NY: Knopf, 1925), 23–30.

Cooperman, Stanley. "The War Lover: Claude (WC)." *World War I and the American Novel* (Baltimore, Md: Johns Hopkins U P, 1967), 129–137. Rpt Murphy (1984).

Cunliffe, Marcus. "The Two or More Worlds of WC." Slote & Faulkner, 21–42.

Donovan, Josephine. *After the Fall: The Demeter-Persephone Myth in Wharton, C, and Glasgow* (University Park: Penn State U P, 1988), 85–127.

Douglas, Ann. "WC: A Problematic Ideal." *Women, the Arts, and the 1920s in Paris and New York,* ed Kenneth W Wheeler & Virginia Lee Lussier (New Brunswick, NJ: Transaction, 1982), 14–19.

*Edel, Leon. "Psychoanalysis." *Literary Biography* (Garden City, NY: Doubleday, 1959), 91–122. Augmented as "A Cave of One's Own." *Stuff of Sleep and Dreams* by Edel (NY: Harper & Row, 1982).

Fetterley, Judith. "*My Ántonia,* Jim Burden and the Dilemma of the Lesbian Writer." *Gender Studies: New Directions in Feminist Criticism,* ed Judith Spector (Bowling Green, Ohio: Bowling Green State U Popular P, 1986), 43–59.

Gelfant, Blanche H. "Movement and Melody: The Disembodiment of Lucy Gayheart." *Women Writing in America* (Hanover, NH: U P New England, 1984), 117–143.

Giannone, Richard. "WC and the Human Voice." Murphy (1974), 21–49.

Gilbert, Sandra M & Susan Gubar. "Lighting Out for the Territories: WC's Lost Horizons." *No Man's Land: The Place of the Woman Writer in the Twentieth Century,* Vol 2 (New Haven, Conn: Yale U P, 1989), 169–212.

Gwin, Minrose C. "Sapphira and Her Slave Women: C and Her Problematic South." *Black and White Women of the Old South* (Knoxville: U Tennessee P, 1985), 131–149.

Huf, Linda. "*The Song of the Lark* (1915): The Exception of WC." *A Portrait of the Artist as a Young Woman* (NY: Ungar, 1983), 80–102.

Jessup, Josephine Lurie. "WC: Tutelary Patroness." *The Faith of Our Feminists: A Study in the Novels of Edith Wharton, Ellen Glasgow, WC* (NY: Smith, 1950), 54–75, passim.

Knopf, Alfred A. "Miss C." Slote & Faulkner, 205–224.

Love, Glen A. "The Cowboy in the Laboratory: WC's Hesitant Moderns." *New Americans: The Westerner and the Modern Experience in the American Novel* (Lewisburg, Pa: Bucknell U P, 1982), 107–169.

Mencken, H L. "WC." *The Borzoi 1920,* ed Alfred Knopf (NY: Knopf, 1920), 28–31.

Miller, James E, Jr. "WC and the Art of Fiction." Slote & Faulkner, 121–148.

Morgan, H Wayne. "WC: The Artist's Quest." *Writers in Transition* (NY: Hill & Wang, 1963), 60–81.

Murphy, John J. "A Comprehensive View of C's O Pioneers!" Murphy (1984), 113–127.

Murphy & Kevin A Synnott. "The Recognition of WC's Art." Murphy (1984), 1–28.

Nichols, Kathleen L. "The Celibate Male in *A Lost Lady:* The Unreliable Center of Consciousness." Murphy (1984), 186–197.

O'Brien, Sharon. "Mothers, Daughters, and the 'Art Necessity': WC and the Creative Process." *American Novelists Revisited,* ed Fritz Fleischmann (Boston: Hall, 1982), 265–298.

Perez, Carlos A. "'Paul's Case': The Outsider." *Youth Suicide Prevention: Lessons From Literature,* ed Sara Munson Deats & Lagretta Tallent Lenker (NY: Plenum, 1989), 135–154.

Porter, Katherine Anne. "Critical Reflections on WC." *The Troll Garden* (NY: NAL, 1961), 139–151.

Quirk, Tom. "Fragments of Desire," "The Road Home." *Bergson and American Culture: The Worlds of WC and Wallace Stevens* (Chapel Hill: U North Carolina P, 1990), 97–179.

Randall, John H, III. "WC and the Pastoral Tradition." Murphy (1974), 75–96.

Romines, Ann. *The Home Plot: Women Writing and the Domestic Ritual* (Amherst: U Massachusetts P, 1992), 128–191.

*Rose, Phyllis. "Modernism: The Case of WC." *Modernism Reconsidered,* ed Robert Kiely (Cambridge: Harvard U P, 1983), 123–145.

*Slote, Bernice. "WC and Her First Book." *April Twilights (1903)* (Lincoln: U Nebraska P, 1968), ix–xlv.

Slote. "Introduction." *Uncle Valentine and Other Stories,* ix–xxx.

Slote. "WC: The Secret Web." Murphy (1974), 1–19.

*Slote. "Introduction." *Alexander's Bridge* (Lincoln: U Nebraska P, 1977), v–xxvi. Rpt Murphy (1984).

Snell, George. "Edith Wharton and WC: The James Influence." *The Shapers of American Fiction, 1798–1947* (NY: Dutton, 1947), 140–156.

Stouck, David. "WC and the Impressionistic Novel." Murphy (1984), 48–66.

Stout, Janis P. "The Duplicitous Art of WC." *Strategies of Reticence: Silence and Meaning in the Works of Jane Austen, WC, Katherine Anne Porter, and Joan Didion* (Charlottesville: U P Virginia, 1990), 66–111.

Sutherland, Donald. "WC: The Classic Voice." Slote & Faulkner, 156–179. Rpt Bloom (1985).

Trilling, Lionel. "WC." *After the Genteel Tradition,* ed Malcolm Cowley (NY: Norton, 1937), 52–63. Rpt Bloom (1985).

*Van Antwerp, Margaret A, ed. "WC." *Dictionary of Literary Biography Documentary Series,* Vol 1 (Detroit: Bruccoli Clark/Gale, 1982), 57–104.

Wagenknecht, Edward. "WC and the Lovely Past." *Cavalcade of the American Novel* (NY: Holt, 1952), 319–338.

*Welty, Eudora. "The House of WC." Slote & Faulkner, 3–20. Rpt Murphy (1984), Bloom (1985).

West, Rebecca. "The Classic Artist." *The Strange Necessity* (Garden City, NY: Doubleday, Doran, 1928), 233–248. Rpt Schroeter.

Woodress, James. "WC: American Experience and European Tradition." Slote & Faulkner, 43–62.

Woodress. "C and Her Friends." Murphy (1984), 81–95.

Woodress. "The Composition of *The Professor's House.*" *Writing the American Classics,* ed James Barbour & Tom Quirk (Chapel Hill: U North Carolina P, 1990), 106–124.

Zabel, Morton Dauwen. "WC: The Tone of Time." *Craft and Character* (NY: Viking, 1957), 264–275. Rpt Bloom (1985).

ARTICLES

Ammons, Elizabeth. "The Engineer as Cultural Hero and WC's First Novel, *Alexander's Bridge.*" *American Quarterly,* 38 (Winter 1986), 746–760.

Arnold, Marilyn. "The Function of Structure in C's *The Professor's House.*" *Colby Library Quarterly,* 11 (Sep 1975), 169–178.

Arnold. "Coming WC!" *Women's Studies,* 11, no 3 (1984), 247–260.

Arnold. "'Of Human Bondage': C's Subnarrative in *Sapphira and the Slave Girl.*" *Mississippi Quarterly,* 40 (Summer 1987), 323–338.

Bailey, Jennifer. "The Dangers of Femininity in WC's Fiction." *Journal of American Studies,* 16 (Dec 1982), 391–406.

Baker, Bruce P, II. "*O Pioneers!:* The Problem of Structure." *Great Plains Quarterly,* 2 (Fall 1982), 218–223.

Bash, James R. "WC and the Anathema of Materialism." *Colby Library Quarterly,* 10 (Sep 1973), 157–168.

Bennett, Mildred R. "The Childhood Worlds of WC." *Great Plains Quarterly,* 2 (Fall 1982), 204–209.

Bennett, S M. "Ornament and Environment: Uses of Folklore in WC's Fiction." *Tennessee Folklore Society Bulletin,* 40 (Sep 1974), 95–102.

Bohlke, L Brent. "Beginnings: WC and 'The Clemency of the Court.'" *Prairie Schooner,* 48 (Summer 1974), 134–144.

Bohlke. "The Ecstasy of Alexandra Bergson." *Colby Library Quarterly,* 11 (Sep 1975), 139–149.

Borgman, Paul. "The Dialectic of WC's Moral Vision." *Renascence,* 27 (Spring 1975), 145–159.

Bradford, Curtis. "WC's Uncollected Short Stories." *American Literature*, 26 (Jan 1955), 537–551.

Brunauer, Dalma H & June Davis Klamecki. "Myra Henshawe's Mortal Enemy." *Christianity and Literature*, 25 (Fall 1975), 7–40.

Bush, Sargent, Jr. "*Shadows on the Rock* and WC's View of the Past." *Queen's Quarterly*, 76 (Summer 1969), 269–285.

Chaliff, Cynthia. "The Art of WC's Craft." *Papers on Language and Literature*, 14 (Winter 1978), 61–73.

Charles, Sister Peter Damian. "*Death Comes for the Archbishop:* A Novel of Love & Death." *New Mexico Quarterly*, 36 (Winter 1966–1967), 389–403.

Charles. "*My Ántonia:* A Dark Dimension." *Western American Literature*, 2 (Summer 1967), 91–108.

Charles. "*The Professor's House:* An Abode of Love and Death." *Colby Library Quarterly*, 8 (Jun 1968), 70–82.

Cherny, Robert W. "WC and the Populists." *Great Plains Quarterly*, 3 (Fall 1983), 206–218.

Comeau, Paul. "The Fool Figure in WC's Fiction." *Western American Literature*, 15 (Winter 1981), 265–278.

Comeau. "WC's *Lucy Gayheart:* A Long Perspective." *Prairie Schooner*, 55 (Spring–Summer 1981), 199–209.

Crane, Joan St C. "WC's Corrections in the Text of *Death Comes for the Archbishop*, 1927 to 1945." *Papers of the Bibliographical Society of America*, 74, no 2 (1980), 117–131.

Curtin, William M. "WC: Individualism and Style." *Colby Library Quarterly*, 8 (Jun 1968), 37–55.

Curtin. "WC and the *Varieties of Religious Experience.*" *Renascence*, 27 (Spring 1975), 115–123.

Ditsky, John. "'Listening With Supersensual Ear': Music in the Novels of WC." *Journal of Narrative Technique*, 13 (Fall 1983), 154–163.

Fischer, Mike. "Pastoralism and Its Discontents: WC and the Burden of Imperialism." *Mosaic*, 23 (Winter 1990), 31–44.

Fox, Maynard. "Symbolic Representation in WC's *O Pioneers!*" *Western American Literature*, 9 (Fall 1974), 187–196.

*Gelfant, Blanche H. "The Forgotten Reaping-Hook: Sex in *My Ántonia.*" *American Literature*, 43 (Mar 1971), 60–82. Rpt Murphy (1984), Bloom (1985), Bloom (1987).

Giannone. "WC and the Unfinished Drama of Deliverance." *Prairie Schooner*, 52 (Spring 1978), 25–46.

*Giltrow, Janet & David Stouck. "WC and a Grammar for Things 'Not Named.'" *Style*, 26 (Spring 1992), 91–113.

Gleason, John B. "The 'Case' of WC." *Western American Literature*, 20 (Winter 1986), 275–299.

Goodman, Charlotte. "The Lost Brother, the Twin: Women Novelists and the Male-Female *Bildungsroman*." *Novel*, 17 (Fall 1983), 28–43.

Greene, George. "*Death Comes for the Archbishop*." *New Mexico Quarterly*, 27 (Spring–Summer 1957), 69–82.

Greene. "WC at Mid-Century." *Thought*, 32 (Winter 1957–1958), 577–592.

Griffiths, Frederick T. "The Woman Warrior: WC and *One of Ours*." *Women's Studies*, 11, no 3 (1984), 261–285.

Grumbach, Doris. "A Study of the Small Room in *The Professor's House*." *Women's Studies*, 11, no 3 (1984), 327–345.

Hamner, Eugénie Lambert. "The Unknown, Well-Known Child in C's Last Novel." *Women's Studies*, 11, no 3 (1984), 347–357.

Harrell, David. "'We Contacted Smithsonian': The Wetherills at Mesa Verde." *New Mexico Historical Review*, 62 (Jul 1987), 229–248.

Helmick, Evelyn Thomas. "The Broken World: Medievalism in *A Lost Lady*." *Renascence*, 28 (Autumn 1975), 39–46. Rpt Murphy (1984).

Helmick. "The Mysteries of Ántonia." *Midwest Quarterly*, 17 (Winter 1976), 173–185. Rpt Bloom (1987).

*Hicks, Granville. "The Case Against WC." *English Journal*, 22 (Nov 1933), 703–710.

Kubitschek, Missy Dehn. "St. Peter and the World All Before Him." *Western American Literature*, 17 (Spring 1982), 13–20.

Lambert, Deborah G. "The Defeat of a Hero: Autonomy and Sexuality in *My Ántonia*." *American Literature*, 53 (Jan 1982), 676–690. Rpt Bloom (1987).

Leddy, Michael. "Observation and Narration in WC's *Obscure Destinies*." *Studies in American Fiction*, 16 (Autumn 1988), 141–153.

Love, Glen A. "*The Professor's House*: C, Hemingway, and the Chastening of American Prose Style." *Western American Literature*, 24 (Feb 1990), 295–311.

*Martin, Terence. "The Drama of Memory in *My Ántonia*." *PMLA*, 84 (Mar 1969), 304–311. Rpt Bloom (1987).

Maxfield, James F. "Strategies of Self-Deception in WC's *The Professor's House*." *Studies in the Novel*, 16 (Spring 1984), 72–86.

McGill, Robert Alan. "Heartbreak: Western Enchantment and Western Fact in WC's *The Professor's House*." *South Dakota Review*, 16 (Autumn 1978), 56–79.

Mencken, H L. "Sunrise on the Prairie." *Smart Set,* 58 (Feb 1919), 138–144. Rpt Schroeter.

Michaels, Walter Benn. "The Vanishing American." *American Literary History,* 2 (Summer 1990), 220–241.

*Miller, James E, Jr. *"My Ántonia:* A Frontier Drama of Time." *American Quarterly,* 10 (Winter 1958), 476–484. Rpt Bloom (1987).

Miller. *"My Ántonia* and the American Dream." *Prairie Schooner,* 48 (Summer 1974), 112–123.

Morrow, Nancy. "WC's *A Lost Lady* and the Nineteenth Century Novel of Adultery." *Women's Studies,* 11, no 3 (1984), 287–303.

Moseley, Ann. "The Dual Nature of Art in *The Song of the Lark." Western American Literature,* 14 (Spring 1979), 19–32.

Murphy, John J. "WC's Archbishop: A Western and Classical Perspective." *Western American Literature,* 13 (Summer 1978), 141–150. Rpt Bloom (1985).

*Murphy. "WC and Religion: Highway to the World and Beyond." *Literature and Belief,* 4 (1984), 49–68.

O'Brien, Sharon. "The Unity of WC's 'Two-Part Pastoral': Passion in *O Pioneers!" Studies in American Fiction,* 6 (Autumn 1978), 157–171.

O'Brien. "'The Thing Not Named': WC as a Lesbian Writer." *Signs,* 9 (Summer 1984), 576–599.

*O'Connor, Margaret Anne. "A Guide to the Letters of WC." *Resources for American Literary Study,* 4 (Autumn 1974), 145–172.

Panill, Linda. "WC's Artist-Heroines." *Women's Studies,* 11, no 3 (1984), 223–232.

Peck, Demaree. "Thea Kronborg's 'Song of Myself': The Artist's Imaginative Inheritance in *The Song of the Lark." Western American Literature,* 26 (May 1991), 21–38.

Piacentino, Edward J. "Another Angle of WC's Artistic Prism: Impressionistic Character Portraiture in *My Ántonia." Midamerica,* 9 (1982), 53–64.

Pulsipher, Jenny Hale. "Expatriation and Reconciliation: The Pilgrimage Tradition in *Sapphira and the Slave Girl." Literature and Belief,* 8 (1988), 89–100.

Quirk, Tom. "Fitzgerald and C: *The Great Gatsby." American Literature,* 54 (Dec 1982), 576–591.

Romines, Ann. "After the Christmas Tree: WC and Domestic Ritual." *American Literature,* 60 (Mar 1988), 61–82.

Rosowski, Susan J. "The Pattern of WC's Novels." *Western American Literature,* 15 (Winter 1981), 243–263.

Rosowski. "WC's *A Lost Lady*: Art Versus the Closing Frontier." *Great Plains Quarterly,* 2 (Fall 1982), 239–248.

Rosowski. "WC's Female Landscapes: *The Song of the Lark* and *Lucy Gayheart.*" *Women's Studies,* 11, no 3 (1984), 233–246.

Rosowski. "Writing Against Silences: Female Adolescent Development in the Novels of WC." *Studies in the Novel,* 21 (Spring 1989), 60–77.

Rosowski & Bernice Slote. "WC's 1916 Mesa Verde Essay: The Genesis of *The Professor's House.*" *Prairie Schooner,* 58 (Winter 1984), 81–92.

Rucker, Mary E. "Prospective Focus in *My Ántonia.*" *Arizona Quarterly,* 29 (Winter 1973), 303–316.

Ryan, Maureen. "No Woman's Land: Gender in WC's *One of Ours.*" *Studies in American Fiction,* 18 (Spring 1990), 65–75.

Schach, Paul. "Russian Wolves in Folktales and Literature of the Plains: A Question of Origins." *Great Plains Quarterly,* 3 (Spring 1983), 67–78.

Schneider, Sister Lucy. "Artistry and Instinct: WC's 'Land-Philosophy.'" *College Language Association Journal,* 16 (Jun 1973), 485–504.

Schroeter, James. "WC and *The Professor's House.*" *Yale Review,* 54 (Jun 1965), 494–512. Rpt Schroeter.

Schwind, Jean. "The 'Beautiful' War in *One of Ours.*" *Modern Fiction Studies,* 30 (Spring 1984), 53–71.

*Schwind. "The Benda Illustrations to *My Ántonia*: C's Silent Supplement to Jim Burden's Narrative." *PMLA,* 100 (Jan 1985), 51–67.

Skaggs, Merrill Maguire. "WC's Experimental Southern Novel." *Mississippi Quarterly,* 35 (Winter 1981–1982), 3–14.

Skaggs. "*Death Comes for the Archbishop*: C's Mystery and Manners." *American Literature,* 57 (Oct 1985), 395–406.

Skaggs. "Death in C Major: WC's Perilous Journey Toward the Ordinary in *Lucy Gayheart.*" *Literature and Belief,* 8 (1988), 76–88.

Slote, Bernice. "WC Reports Chautauqua, 1894." *Prairie Schooner,* 43 (Spring 1969), 117–128.

*Stewart, David H. "C's Mortal Comedy." *Queen's Quarterly,* 73 (Summer 1966), 244–259.

Stineback, David C. "WC's Ironic Masterpiece." *Arizona Quarterly,* 29 (Winter 1973), 317–330.

Stouck, David. "Perspective as Structure and Theme in *My Ántonia.*" *Texas Studies in Literature and Language,* 12 (Summer 1970), 285–294. Rpt Bloom (1987).

Stouck. "*O Pioneers!*: WC and the Epic Imagination." *Prairie Schooner,* 46 (Spring 1972), 23–34.

Stouck. "WC and *The Professor's House:* 'Letting Go With the Heart.'" *Western American Literature,* 7 (Spring 1972), 13–24.

Stouck. "C's Archbishop and Travel Writing." *Western American Literature,* 17 (Spring 1982), 3–12.

Stouck, Mary-Ann & David. "Art and Religion in *Death Comes for the Archbishop.*" *Arizona Quarterly,* 29 (Winter 1973), 293–302.

Stout, Janis P. "Autobiography as Journey in *The Professor's House.*" *Studies in American Fiction,* 19 (Autumn 1991), 203–215.

Strychacz, Thomas F. "The Ambiguities of Escape in WC's *The Professor's House.*" *Studies in American Fiction,* 14 (Spring 1986), 49–61.

Swift, John N. "Memory, Myth, and *The Professor's House.*" *Western American Literature,* 20 (Winter 1986), 301–314.

Tanner, Stephen L. "Seeking and Finding in C's *My Mortal Enemy.*" *Literature and Belief,* 8 (1988), 27–38.

Urgo, Joseph R. "How Context Determines Fact: Historicism in WC's *A Lost Lady.*" *Studies in American Fiction,* 17 (Autumn 1989), 183–192.

Wasserman, Loretta. "The Lovely Storm: Sexual Initiation in Two Early WC Novels." *Studies in the Novel,* 14 (Winter 1982), 348–358.

Wasserman. "WC's 'The Old Beauty' Reconsidered." *Studies in American Fiction,* 16 (Autumn 1988), 217–227.

Whaley, Elizabeth Gates. "C's *My Mortal Enemy.*" *Prairie Schooner,* 48 (Summer 1974), 124–133.

Wiesenthal, C Susan. "Female Sexuality in WC's *O Pioneers!* and the Era of Scientific Sexology: A Dialogue Between Frontiers." *Ariel,* 21 (Jan 1990), 41–63.

Wild, Barbara. "'The Thing Not Named' in *The Professor's House.*" *Western American Literature* 12 (Winter 1978), 263–274.

Woodress, James. "WC and History." *Arizona Quarterly,* 34 (Autumn 1978), 239–254.

Woodress. "The Uses of Biography: The Case of WC." *Great Plains Quarterly,* 2 (Fall 1982), 195–203.

Work, James C. "WC's Archbishop and the Seven Deadly Sins." *Platte Valley Review,* 14 (Spring 1986), 93–103.

*Yongue, Patricia Lee. "WC's Aristocrats." *Southern Humanities Review,* 14 (Winter–Spring 1980), 43–56, 111–125.

— *James Woodress*

KATE CHOPIN

St Louis, Mo, 8 Feb 1851–St Louis, Mo, 22 Aug 1904

During her lifetime, Kate Chopin won national fame as a local colorist for her two short-story collections and gained national infamy for her "immoral" novel *The Awakening*. At the time of her death, Chopin was remembered primarily as a regional writer who characterized Louisiana Creoles and Cajuns in vivid detail. In the late 1960s and early 1970s Per Seyersted's *Critical Biography* and *Complete Works* stirred reassessment of Chopin as an important American writer. Since the 1970s the popularity and critical reputation of her writings have grown. Chopin's works have become the subjects for an array of critical approaches, drawing the interest in particular of students of American literary realism and of feminist critics.

Bibliographies

* "Bibliographic Essay: A Guide to the Literary Works By and About KC." Bonner, *The KC Companion*, 233–245.

Bibliography of American Literature, comp Jacob Blanck. New Haven, Conn: Yale U P, 1955–1991. Primary.

Bonner, Thomas, Jr. "KC: An Annotated Bibliography." *Bulletin of Bibliography*, 32 (Jul–Sep 1975), 101–105. Primary & secondary.

Gannon, Barbara C. "KC, a Secondary Bibliography." *American Literary Realism*, 17 (Spring 1984), 124–129.

*Pope, Deborah. "Recent Developments in KC Studies." *University of Mississippi Studies in English*, 8 (1990), 254–258. Secondary.

Potter, Richard H. "KC and Her Critics: An Annotated Checklist." *Missouri Historical Society Bulletin*, 26 (Jul 1970), 306–317. Secondary.

Springer, Marlene. *Edith Wharton and KC: A Reference Guide*. Boston: Hall, 1976. Secondary.

Springer. "KC: A Reference Guide Updated." *Resources for American Literary Study*, 11 (Autumn 1981), 281–303. Secondary.

*Wagner-Martin, Linda. "Recent Books on KC." *Mississippi Quarterly,* 42 (Spring 1989), 193–196. Secondary.

Books

At Fault. St Louis: Nixon-Jones, 1890. Novel.

Bayou Folk. Boston & NY: Houghton, Mifflin, 1894. Stories.

A Night in Acadie. Chicago: Way & Williams, 1897. Stories.

The Awakening. Chicago & NY: Stone, 1899. Novel.

A KC Miscellany, ed Per Seyersted & Emily Toth. Oslo: Universitetsforlaget / Natchitoches, La: Northwestern State U P, 1979.

Editions & Collections

The Complete Works of KC, 2 vols, ed Per Seyersted. Baton Rouge: Louisiana State U P, 1970.

KC: The Awakening and Other Stories, ed with intro by Lewis Leary. NY: Holt, Rinehart & Winston, 1970.

The Storm and Other Stories by KC With The Awakening, ed with intro by Seyersted. Old Westbury, NY: Feminist, 1974.

The Awakening: An Authoritative Text, Contexts, Criticism, ed with intro by Margaret Culley. NY: Norton, 1976.

A Vocation and a Voice, ed with intro by Emily Toth. NY: Penguin, 1991.

Manuscripts & Archives

Missouri Historical Society, St Louis.

Biographies

BOOKS

*Seyersted, Per. *KC: A Critical Biography.* Oslo: Universitetsforlaget / Baton Rouge: Louisiana State U P, 1969.

Toth, Emily. *KC.* NY: Morrow, 1990.

ARTICLES

Schuyler, William. "KC." *Writer,* 7 (Aug 1894), 115–117.

Toth, Emily. "Some Problems in KC Scholarship." *Kate Chopin Newsletter,* 1 (Fall 1975), 30–33.

Toth. "KC Remembered." *Kate Chopin Newsletter,* 1 (Winter 1975–1976), 21–27.

Toth. "The Shadow of the First Biographer: The Case of KC." *Southern Review,* 26 (Spring 1990), 285–292.

Critical Studies

BOOKS

*Bonner, Thomas, Jr. *The KC Companion.* NY: Greenwood, 1988. Includes KC's translations of French fiction.

*Ewell, Barbara C. *KC.* NY: Ungar, 1986.

Hoder-Salmon, Marilyn. *KC's The Awakening: Screenplay as Interpretation.* Gainesville: U P Florida, 1992.

*Papke, Mary E. *Verging on the Abyss: The Social Fiction of KC and Edith Wharton.* NY: Greenwood, 1990.

Rankin, Daniel S. *KC and Her Creole Stories.* Philadelphia: U Pennsylvania P, 1932.

*Skaggs, Peggy. *KC.* NY: Twayne, 1985.

COLLECTIONS OF ESSAYS

Bloom, Harold, ed. *KC.* NY: Chelsea House, 1986.

Boren, Lynda S & Sara deSaussure Davis, eds. *KC Reconsidered: Beyond the Bayou.* Baton Rouge: Louisiana State U P, 1992.

Koloski, Bernard, ed. *Approaches to Teaching KC's The Awakening.* NY: MLA, 1988.

*Martin, Wendy, ed. *New Essays on The Awakening.* NY: Cambridge U P, 1988.

SPECIAL JOURNALS

Kate Chopin Newsletter (triquarterly, 1975— Winter 1976–1977).
Louisiana Studies, 14 (Spring 1975). KC issue.

BOOK SECTIONS

*Arms, George. "KC's *The Awakening* in the Perspective of Her Literary Career." *Essays on American Literature in Honor of Jay B. Hubbell,* ed Clarence Gohdes (Durham, NC: Duke U P, 1967), 215–228.

*Showalter, Elaine. "Tradition and the Female Talent: *The Awakening* as a Solitary Book." Martin, 33–58. Rpt *Sister's Choice: Tradition and Change in American Women's Writing* by Showalter (Oxford, UK: Clarendon, 1991).

ARTICLES

Anastasopoulou, Maria. "Rites of Passage in KC's *The Awakening.*" *Southern Literary Journal,* 23 (Spring 1991), 19–30.

*Arner, Robert. "KC." *Louisiana Studies,* 14 (Spring 1975), 11–139.

Brown, Pearl L. "KC's Fiction: Order and Disorder in a Stratified Society." *University of Mississippi Studies in English,* 9 (1991), 119–134.

Dyer, Joyce Coyne. "Night Images in the Works of KC." *American Literary Realism,* 14 (Autumn 1981), 216–230.

Eble, Kenneth. "A Forgotten Novel: KC's *The Awakening.*" *Western Humanities Review,* 10 (Summer 1956), 261–269. Rpt *The Awakening: An Authoritative Text, Contexts, Criticism.*

Fletcher, Marie. "The Southern Woman in the Fiction of KC." *Louisiana History,* 7 (Spring 1966), 117–132.

Fluck, Winfried. "Tentative Transgressions: KC's Fiction as a Mode of Symbolic Action." *Studies in American Fiction,* 10 (Autumn 1982), 151–171.

Kearns, Katherine. "The Nullification of Edna Pontellier." *American Literature,* 63 (Mar 1991), 62–88.

Lattin, Patricia Hopkins. "KC's Repeating Characters." *Mississippi Quarterly,* 33 (Winter 1979–1980), 19–37.

Lattin. "The Search for Self in KC's Fiction: Simple Versus Complex Vision." *Southern Studies,* 21 (Summer 1982), 222–235.

Leary, Lewis. "KC's Other Novel." *Southern Literary Journal,* 1 (Dec 1968), 60–74.

Malzahn, Manfred. "The Strange Demise of Edna Pontellier." *Southern Literary Journal,* 23 (Spring 1991), 31–39.

Radcliff-Umstead, Douglas. "Literature of Deliverance: Images of Nature in *The Awakening.*" *Southern Studies,* ns 1 (Summer 1990), 127–147.

*Ringe, Donald A. "Romantic Imagery in KC's *The Awakening.*" *American Literature,* 43 (Jan 1972), 580–588. Rpt *The Awakening: An Authoritative Text, Contexts, Criticism.*

Ringe. "Cane River World: KC's *At Fault* and Related Stories." *Studies in American Fiction,* 3 (Autumn 1975), 157–166.

Schweitzer, Ivy. "Maternal Discourse and the Romance of Self-Possession in KC's *The Awakening.*" *Boundary 2,* 17 (Spring 1990), 158–186.

Seyersted, Per. "KC: An Important St. Louis Writer Reconsidered." *Missouri Historical Society Bulletin,* 19 (Jan 1963), 89–114.

Skaggs, Peggy. "Three Tragic Figures in KC's *The Awakening.*" *Louisiana Studies,* 13 (Winter 1974), 345–364.

Thomas, Heather Kirk. "'Development of the Literary West': An Undiscovered KC Essay." *American Literary Realism,* 22 (Winter 1990), 69–75.

Toth, Emily. "The Independent Woman and 'Free' Love." *Massachusetts Review,* 16 (Autumn 1975), 647–664.

*Toth. "KC's *The Awakening* as Feminist Criticism." *Louisiana Studies,* 15 (Fall 1976), 241–251.

Toth. "KC and Literary Convention: 'Desiree's Baby.'" *Southern Studies,* 20 (Summer 1981), 201–208.

Toth. "KC on Divine Love and Suicide: Two Rediscovered Articles." *American Literature,* 63 (Mar 1991), 115–121.

*Wolff, Cynthia Griffin. "Thanatos and Eros: KC's *The Awakening.*" *American Quarterly,* 25 (Oct 1973), 449–471. Rpt *The Awakening: An Authoritative Text, Contexts, Criticism.*

Wolff. "KC and the Fiction of Limits: 'Desiree's Baby.'" *Southern Literary Journal,* 10 (Spring 1978), 123–133.

— Sandra L. Ballard

CARSON MCCULLERS
Columbus, Ga, 19 Feb 1917–Nyack, NY, 29 Sep 1967

Although Carson McCullers's first novel, *The Heart Is a Lonely Hunter,* created a literary sensation, her later works were less well received. The play version of *The Member of the Wedding* solidified her popular success, but it was not until the publication of the Omnibus collection of her work that she received significant critical attention. Since McCullers's death she has been favorably compared with other figures of the Southern Renascence. Feminist critics, in particular, have found much to explore and admire in McCullers's work.

Bibliographies

*Carr, Virginia Spencer "CM." *Contemporary Authors Bibliographical Series: American Novelists,* ed James J Martine (Detroit: Bruccoli Clark/Gale, 1986), 293–345. Primary & secondary; includes essay on secondary sources.

Kiernan, Robert F. *Katherine Anne Porter and CM: A Reference Guide.* Boston: Hall, 1976. Secondary.

*Shapiro, Adrian M, Jackson R Bryer & Kathleen Field. *CM: A Descriptive Listing and Annotated Bibliography of Criticism.* NY: Garland, 1980. Primary & secondary.

Books

The Heart Is a Lonely Hunter. Boston: Houghton Mifflin, 1940. Novel.

Reflections in a Golden Eye. Boston: Houghton Mifflin, 1941. Novel.

The Member of the Wedding. Boston: Houghton Mifflin, 1946. Novel.

The Member of the Wedding. NY: New Directions, 1951. Play.

The Ballad of the Sad Café: The Novels and Stories of CM. Boston: Houghton Mifflin, 1951; *The Ballad of the Sad Café: The Shorter Novels and Stories of CM.* London: Cresset, 1952.

The Square Root of Wonderful. Boston: Houghton Mifflin, 1958. Repub with "A Personal Preface" by CM, Dunwoody, Ga: Berg. 1971. Play.

Collected Short Stories and the Novel The Ballad of the Sad Café. Boston: Houghton Mifflin, 1961.

Clock Without Hands. Boston: Houghton Mifflin, 1961. Novel.

Sweet as a Pickle and Clean as a Pig. Boston: Houghton Mifflin, 1964. Children's verse.

The Mortgaged Heart, ed with intro by Margarita G Smith. Boston: Houghton Mifflin, 1971. Fiction, nonfiction & poems.

Edition & Collection

The Heart Is a Lonely Hunter. Birmingham, Ala: Oxmoor, 1984. Includes pamphlet intro by Virginia Spencer Carr.

Collected Stories of CM: Including The Member of the Wedding and The Ballad of the Sad Café, ed with intro by Carr. Boston: Houghton Mifflin, 1987.

Manuscripts & Archives

The major collections are at the Harry Ransom Humanities Research Center, U of Texas, Austin, & Duke U Library.

Biographies

BOOKS

*Carr, Virginia Spencer. *The Heart Is a Lonely Hunter: A Biography of CM.* Garden City, NY: Doubleday, 1975.

*Evans, Oliver. *CM: Her Life and Work.* London: Owen, 1965. Repub as *The Ballad of CM.* NY: Coward-McCann, 1966.

Critical Studies

BOOKS

*Carr, Virginia Spencer. *Understanding CM*. Columbia: U South Carolina P, 1990.

Cook, Richard. *CM*. NY: Ungar, 1975.

Graver, Lawrence. *CM*. Minneapolis: U Minnesota P, 1969.

*McDowell, Margaret B. *CM*. NY: Twayne, 1980.

*Westling, Louise. *Sacred Groves and Ravaged Gardens: The Fiction of Eudora Welty, CM, and Flannery O'Connor*. Athens: U Georgia P, 1985.

COLLECTION OF ESSAYS

*Bloom, Harold, ed. *CM*. NY: Chelsea House, 1986.

SPECIAL JOURNAL

Pembroke Magazine, 20 (1988). CM issue.

BOOK SECTIONS

Aldridge, Robert. "Two Planetary Systems: *The Heart Is a Lonely Hunter.*" *The Modern American Novel and the Movies*, ed Gerald Peary & Roger Shatzkin (NY: Ungar, 1978), 119–130.

Graver, Lawrence. "CM." *Seven American Women Writers of the Twentieth Century*, ed Maureen Howard (Minneapolis: U Minnesota P, 1977), 265–307.

Gray, Richard J. "Moods and Absences: CM." *The Literature of Memory* (Baltimore, Md: Johns Hopkins U P, 1977), 265–273.

Huf, Linda. "CM's Young Woman With a Great Future Behind Her." *A Portrait of the Artist as a Young Woman* (NY: Ungar, 1983), 104–123.

MacDonald, Edgar E. "The Symbolic Unity of *The Heart Is a Lonely Hunter.*" *A Festschrift for Professor Marguerite Roberts, on the Occasion of Her Retirement From Westhampton College, University of Richmond, Virginia*, ed Frieda Elaine Penninger (Richmond: U Richmond P, 1976), 168–187.

Malin, Irving. "The Gothic Family." *Psychoanalysis and American Fiction,* ed Malin (NY: Dutton, 1965), 255–277.

McBride, Mary. "Loneliness and Longing in Selected Plays of CM and Tennessee Williams." *Modern American Drama: The Female Canon,* ed June Schlueter (Rutherford, NJ: Fairleigh Dickinson U P / London: Associated U P, 1990), 143–150.

Messent, Peter. "Continuity and Change in the Southern Novella." *The Modern American Novella,* ed A Robert Lee (London: Vision / NY: St Martin, 1989), 113–138.

Olauson, Judith. *The American Woman Playwright: A View of Criticism and Characterization* (Troy, NY: Whitston, 1981), 45–75.

Rich, Nancy B. "CM and Human Rights." *A Fair Day in the Affections,* ed Jack Durant & M Thomas Hester (Raleigh, NC: Winston, 1980), 205–212.

Williams, Tennessee. "This Book." *Reflections in a Golden Eye* (Norfolk, Conn: New Directions, 1950), ix–xxi.

ARTICLES

*Baldanza, Frank. "Plato in Dixie." *Georgia Review,* 12 (Summer 1958), 151–167.

Bolsterli, Margaret. "'Bound' Characters in Porter, Welty, and M: The Prerevolutionary Status of Women in American Fiction." *Bucknell Review,* 24, no 1 (1978), 95–105.

*Broughton, Panthea Reid. "Rejection of the Feminine in CM's *The Ballad of the Sad Café*." *Twentieth Century Literature,* 20 (Jan 1974), 34–43.

Buchen, Irving H. "CM: The Case of Convergence." *Bucknell Review,* 21 (Spring 1973), 15–28.

Buchen. "Divine Collusion: The Art of CM." *Dalhousie Review,* 54 (Autumn 1974), 529–541.

*Carr, Virginia Spencer. "CM: Novelist Turned Playwright." *Southern Quarterly,* 25 (Spring 1987), 37–51.

Chamlee, Kenneth D. "Cafés and Community in Three CM Novels." *Studies in American Fiction,* 18 (Autumn 1990), 233–239.

Champion, L. "Black and White Christs in CM's *The Heart Is a Lonely Hunter.*" *Southern Literary Journal,* 24 (Fall 1991), 47–53.

Clark, Charlene. "Selfhood and the Southern Past: A Reading of CM's *Clock Without Hands.*" *Southern Literary Messenger,* 1 (Summer 1975), 16–23.

Dazey, Mary Ann. "Two Voices of the Single Narrator in *The Ballad of the Sad Café.*" *Southern Literary Journal,* 17 (Spring 1985), 33–40.

Dodd, Wayne D. "The Development of Theme Through Symbol in the Novels of CM." *Georgia Review,* 17 (Summer 1963), 206–213.

*Emerson, Donald. "The Ambiguities of *Clock Without Hands.*" *Wisconsin Studies in Contemporary Literature,* 3 (Fall 1962), 15–28.

Evans, Oliver. "The Case of the Silent Singer: A Revaluation of *The Heart Is a Lonely Hunter.*" *Georgia Review,* 19 (Summer 1965), 188–203.

Friedman, Melvin J. "*The Mortgaged Heart:* The Workshop of CM." *Revue des Langues Vivantes,* 42 (US Bicentennial Issue 1976), 143–155.

*Fuller, Janice. "The Conventions of Counterpoint and Fugue in *The Heart Is a Lonely Hunter.*" *Mississippi Quarterly,* 41 (Winter 1987–1988), 55–67.

Gaillard, Dawson F. "The Presence of the Narrator in CM's *Ballad of the Sad Café.*" *Mississippi Quarterly,* 25 (Fall 1972), 419–427.

Giannetti, Louis D. "*The Member of the Wedding.*" *Literature/Film Quarterly,* 4 (Winter 1976), 28–38.

Griffith, Albert J. "CM's Myth of the Sad Café." *Georgia Review,* 21 (Spring 1967), 46–56.

Hamilton, Alice. "Loneliness and Alienation: The Life and Work of CM." *Dalhousie Review,* 50 (Summer 1970), 215–229.

Hassan, Ihab. "CM: The Alchemy of Love and Aesthetics of Pain." *Modern Fiction Studies,* 5 (Winter 1959–1960), 311–326. Rpt *Radical Innocence* by Hassan (Princeton: Princeton U P, 1961).

Hassan. "The Way Down and Out." *Virginia Quarterly Review,* 39 (Winter 1963), 81–93.

Hatanaka, Takami. "On Albee's 'Faithfulness' in Dramatizing M's Novel: *The Ballad of the Sad Café.*" *Journal of the English Institute,* 5 (1973), 39–65.

Kahane, Claire. "Gothic Mirrors and Feminine Identity." *Centennial Review,* 24 (Winter 1980), 43–64.

Kissel, Susan S. "CM's 'Wunderkind': A Case Study in Female Adolescence." *Kentucky Philological Review,* 6 (1991), 15–20.

Kohler, Dayton. "CM: Variations on a Theme." *College English,* 13 (Oct 1951), 1–8.

Korenman, Joan S. "CM's 'Proletarian Novel.'" *Studies in the Humanities,* 5 (Jan 1976), 8–13.

*Lubbers, Klaus. "The Necessary Order: A Study of Theme and Structure in CM's Fiction." *Jahrbuch für Amerikastudien,* 8 (1963), 187–204.

Madden, David. "The Paradox of the Need for Privacy and the Need for Understanding in CM's *The Heart Is a Lonely Hunter.*" *Literature and Psychology,* 17, nos 2–3 (1967), 128–140.

Madden. "Transfixed Among the Self-Inclined Ruins: CM's *The Mortgaged Heart.*" *Southern Literary Journal,* 5 (Fall 1972), 137–162.

*Mathis, Ray. "*Reflections in a Golden Eye:* Myth Making in American Christianity." *Religion in Life,* 39 (Winter 1970), 545–558.

Millichap, Joseph R. "The Realistic Structure of *The Heart Is a Lonely Hunter.*" *Twentieth Century Literature,* 17 (Jan 1971), 11–17.

Millichap. "CM's Literary Ballad." *Georgia Review,* 27 (Fall 1973), 329–339.

*Millichap. "Distorted Matter and Disjunctive Forms: The Grotesque as Modernist Genre." *Arizona Quarterly,* 33 (Winter 1977), 339–347.

*Paden, Frances Freeman. "Autistic Gestures in *The Heart Is a Lonely Hunter.*" *Modern Fiction Studies,* 28 (Autumn 1982), 453–463.

Perry, Constance M. "CM and the Female *Wunderkind.*" *Southern Literary Journal,* 19 (Fall 1986), 36–45.

*Petry, Alice Hall. "Baby Wilson Redux: M's *The Heart Is a Lonely Hunter.*" *Southern Studies,* 25 (Summer 1986), 196–203.

*Petry. "CM's Precocious 'Wunderkind.'" *Southern Quarterly,* 26 (Spring 1988), 31–39.

Phillips, Robert S. "The Gothic Architecture of *The Member of the Wedding.*" *Renascence,* 16 (Winter 1964), 59–72.

*Phillips. "Freaking Out: The Short Stories of CM." *Southwest Review,* 63 (Winter 1978), 65–73.

Presley, Delma Eugene. "The Moral Function of Distortion in Southern Grotesque." *South Atlantic Bulletin,* 37 (May 1972), 37–46.

Presley. "CM and the South." *Georgia Review,* 28 (Spring 1974), 19–32.

Rechnitz, Robert M. "The Failure of Love: The Grotesque in Two Novels by CM." *Georgia Review,* 22 (Winter 1968), 454–463.

Rich, Nancy B. "The 'Ironic Parable of Fascism' in *The Heart Is a Lonely Hunter.*" *Southern Literary Journal,* 9 (Spring 1977), 108–123.

*Roberts, Mary. "Imperfect Androgyny and Imperfect Love in the Works of CM." *University of Hartford Studies in Literature,* 12 (1980), 73–98.

Robinson, W R. "The Life of CM's Imagination." *Southern Humanities Review,* 2 (Summer 1968), 291–302.

*Rubin, Louis D, Jr. "CM: The Aesthetic of Pain." *Virginia Quarterly Review,* 53 (Spring 1977), 265–283. Rpt *A Gallery of Southerners* by Rubin (Baton Rouge: Louisiana State U P, 1982).

Scott, Mary Etta. "An Existential Everyman." *West Virginia University Philological Papers,* 27 (1981), 82–88.

Segrest, M. "Lines I Dare to Write: Lesbian Writing in the South." *Southern Exposure*, 9 (Summer 1981), 53–55, 57–62.

*Sherrill, Rowland A. "M's *The Heart Is a Lonely Hunter*: The Missing Ego and the Problem of the Norm." *Kentucky Review*, 2 (Feb 1968), 5–17.

*Smith, C Michael. "'A Voice in a Fugue': Characters and Musical Structure in CM's *The Heart Is a Lonely Hunter*." *Modern Fiction Studies*, 25 (Summer 1979), 258–263.

Snider, Clifton. "On Death and Dying: CM's *Clock Without Hands*." *Markham Review*, 11 (Spring 1982), 43–46.

Vickery, John B. "CM: A Map of Love." *Wisconsin Studies in Contemporary Literature*, 1 (Winter 1960), 13–24.

Walker, Sue B. "The Link in the Chain Called Love: A New Look at CM's Novels." *Mark Twain Journal*, 18 (Winter 1976–1977), 8–12.

*Westling, Louise. "CM's Tomboys." *Southern Humanities Review*, 14 (Fall 1980), 339–350.

*Westling. "CM's Amazon Nightmare." *Modern Fiction Studies*, 28 (Autumn 1982), 465–473.

*Wilcox, Earl J. "And Then There Were Four: CM's Place in Southern Literature." *McNeese Review*, 29 (1982–1983), 3–12.

— *Virginia Spencer Carr*

JOYCE CAROL OATES
Lockport, NY, 16 Jun 1938–

Since 1963 Joyce Carol Oates has published more than sixty books: novels, collections of short stories, volumes of poetry, plays, and nonfiction. Her novel *them* won the National Book Award for 1970, and many of her short stories have appeared in the *O. Henry Awards* and *Best American Short Stories* series. Categorized early in her career as a literary naturalist, Oates has in fact used almost every mode to explore the vitality—and the social and personal turmoil—of modern America. During the 1980s she produced a pair of overtly feminist novels, *Solstice* and *Marya: A Life*, and launched a series of experimental "genre" novels (including the gothic romance, the horror novel, the detective novel) designed to examine American history and its impact on the present. Oates has attracted substantial critical attention, much of which attempts to define her place in contemporary American fiction.

Bibliographies

Hiemstra, Anne. "A Bibliography of Writings by JCO," "A Bibliography of Writings About JCO." *American Women Writing Fiction: Memory, Identity, Family, Space,* ed Mickey Pearlman (Lexington: U P Kentucky, 1989), 28–35, 35–40.

*Lercangée, Francine, with preface & annotations by Bruce F Michelson. *JCO: An Annotated Bibliography.* NY: Garland, 1986. Primary & secondary.

Books

By the North Gate. NY: Vanguard, 1963. Stories.

With Shuddering Fall. NY: Vanguard, 1964. Novel.

Upon the Sweeping Flood and Other Stories. NY: Vanguard, 1966.

A Garden of Earthly Delights. NY: Vanguard, 1967. Novel.

Expensive People. NY: Vanguard, 1968. Novel.

Women In Love and Other Poems. NY: Albondocani, 1968.

Anonymous Sins & Other Poems. Baton Rouge: Louisiana State U P, 1969.

them. NY: Vanguard, 1969. Novel.

Cupid & Psyche: A Short Story. NY: Albondocani, 1970.

The Wheel of Love and Other Stories. NY: Vanguard, 1970.

Love and Its Derangements: Poems. Baton Rouge: Louisiana State U P, 1970.

Wonderland: A Novel. NY: Vanguard, 1971. Rev ed, London: Gollancz, 1972.

The Edge of Impossibility: Tragic Forms in Literature. NY: Vanguard, 1972. Criticism.

Marriages and Infidelities: Short Stories. NY: Vanguard, 1972.

Do With Me What You Will. NY: Vanguard, 1973. Novel.

Dreaming America & Other Poems. NY: Aloe, 1973.

A Posthumous Sketch. Los Angeles: Black Sparrow, 1973. Prose poem.

The Hostile Sun: The Poetry of D. H. Lawrence. Los Angeles: Black Sparrow, 1973. Criticism.

Angel Fire: Poems. Baton Rouge: Louisiana State U P, 1973.

Plagiarized Material by Fernandes, "trans" JCO. Los Angeles: Black Sparrow, 1974. Story.

The Hungry Ghosts: Seven Allusive Comedies. Los Angeles: Black Sparrow, 1974. Stories.

Where Are You Going, Where Have You Been? Stories of Young America. Greenwich, Conn: Fawcett, 1974.

Miracle Play. Los Angeles: Black Sparrow, 1974.

New Heaven, New Earth: The Visionary Experience in Literature. NY: Vanguard, 1974. Criticism.

The Goddess and Other Women. NY: Vanguard, 1974. Stories.

The Girl. Cambridge, Mass: Pomegranate, 1974. Story.

The Seduction & Other Stories. Los Angeles: Black Sparrow, 1975.

The Poisoned Kiss and Other Stories From the Portuguese (as by Fernandes/JCO). NY: Vanguard, 1975.

The Assassins: A Book of Hours. NY: Vanguard, 1975. Novel.

The Fabulous Beasts: Poems. Baton Rouge: Louisiana State U P, 1975.

The Blessing. Santa Barbara, Calif: Black Sparrow, 1976. Story.

Crossing the Border: Fifteen Tales. NY: Vanguard, 1976.

Childwold. NY: Vanguard, 1976. Novel.

The Triumph of the Spider Monkey. Santa Barbara, Calif: Black Sparrow, 1976. Story.

Daisy. Santa Barbara, Calif: Black Sparrow, 1977. Story.

Night-Side: Eighteen Tales. NY: Vanguard, 1977.

Season of Peril. Santa Barbara, Calif: Black Sparrow, 1977. Poems.

Women Whose Lives Are Food, Men Whose Lives Are Money: Poems. Baton Rouge & London: Louisiana State U P, 1978.

Son of the Morning: A Novel. NY: Vanguard, 1978.

Sentimental Education. Los Angeles: Sylvester & Orphanos, 1978. Novella.

The Step-Father. Northridge, Calif: Lord John, 1978. Story.

All the Good People I've Left Behind. Santa Barbara, Calif: Black Sparrow, 1979. Stories.

The Lamb of Abyssalia. Cambridge, Mass: Pomegranate, 1979. Story.

Unholy Loves: A Novel. NY: Vanguard, 1979.

Cybele. Santa Barbara, Calif: Black Sparrow, 1979. Novel.

Queen of the Night. Northridge, Calif: Lord John, 1979. Story.

A Middle-Class Education. NY: Albondocani, 1980. Story.

Bellefleur. NY: Robbins/Dutton, 1980. Novel.

A Sentimental Education: Stories. NY: Dutton, 1980.

Three Plays. Princeton, NJ: Ontario Review, 1980.

Celestial Timepiece. Dallas: Pressworks, 1980. Poems.

Contraries: Essays. NY: Oxford U P, 1981.

Angel of Light. NY: Dutton, 1981. Novel.

Nightless Nights: Nine Poems. Concord, NH: Ewert, 1981.

Invisible Woman: New & Selected Poems, 1970–1982. Princeton, NJ: Ontario Review, 1982.

A Bloodsmoor Romance. NY: Dutton, 1982. Novel.

The Metamorphosis. Logan, Iowa: Perfection Form, 1982. Story.

The Profane Art: Essays and Reviews. NY: Dutton 1983.

Funland. Concord, NH: Ewert, 1983. Story.

Mysteries of Winterthurn: A Novel. NY: Dutton, 1984.

Luxury of Sin. Northridge, Calif: Lord John, 1984. Poems.

Last Days: Stories. NY: Dutton, 1984.

Solstice. NY: Abrahams/Dutton, 1985. Novel.

Wild Nights. Athens, Ohio: Croissant, 1985. Story.

Marya: A Life. NY: Abrahams/Dutton, 1986. Novel.

The Miraculous Birth. Concord, NH: Ewert, 1986. Poem.

Raven's Wing. NY: Abraham/Dutton, 1986. Stories.

Blue-Bearded Lover. Concord, NH: Ewert, 1987. Story.

On Boxing. Garden City, NY: Dolphin/Doubleday, 1987. Nonfiction.

You Must Remember This. NY: Abrahams/Dutton, 1987. Novel.

The Time Traveler: Poems. Northridge, Calif: Lord John, 1987. Augmented ed, NY: Abrahams/Dutton, 1989.

Lives of the Twins (as by Rosamond Smith). NY & c: Simon & Schuster, 1987; *Kindred Passions.* London: Collins, 1988. Novel.

The Assignation. NY: Ecco, 1988. Stories.

(Woman) Writer: Occasions and Opportunities. NY: Abrahams/Dutton, 1988. Essays.

American Appetites. NY: Abrahams/Dutton, 1989. Novel.

Soul/Mate (as by Smith). NY: Abrahams/Dutton, 1989. Novel.

Because It Is Bitter, and Because It Is My Heart. NY: Abrahams/Dutton, 1990. Novel.

I Lock My Door Upon Myself. NY: Ecco, 1990. Novel.

Nemesis (as by Smith). NY: Abrahams/Dutton, 1990. Novel.

Oates in Exile. Toronto: Exile, 1990. Stories.

The Rise of Life on Earth. NY: New Directions, 1991. Novel.

Heat and Other Stories. NY: Abrahams/Dutton, 1991.

Twelve Plays. NY: Abrahams/Dutton, 1991.

Black Water. NY: Abrahams/Dutton, 1992. Novel.

Where Is Here? Hopewell, NJ: Ecco, 1992. Stories.

Snake Eyes (as by Smith). NY: Abrahams/Dutton, 1992. Novel.

Other

Scenes From American Life: Contemporary Short Fiction, ed JCO. NY: Vanguard, 1973.

Ontario Review (Fall 1974–), ed JCO & Raymond J Smith.

The Best American Short Stories, 1979, ed JCO & Shannon Ravenel. Boston: Houghton Mifflin, 1979.

Night Walks: A Bedside Companion, ed JCO. Princeton, NJ: Ontario Review, 1982, Miscellany.

First Person Singular: Writers on Their Craft, ed JCO. Princeton, NJ: Ontario Review, 1983. Essays & interviews.

Story: Fictions Past and Present, ed JCO & Boyd Litzinger. Lexington, Mass & Toronto: Heath, 1985.

Reading the Fights, ed JCO & Daniel Halpern. NY: Holt, 1988. Miscellany.

The Best American Essays, 1991, ed JCO & Robert Atwan. NY: Ticknor & Fields, 1991.

The Sophisticated Cat: A Gathering of Stories, Poems, and Miscellaneous Writings About Cats, ed JCO & Halpern. NY: Abrahams/Dutton, 1992.

Collection

Love and Its Derangements and Other Poems, Comprising Anonymous Sins and Other Poems, Love and Its Derangements, and Angel Fire. Greenwich, Conn: Fawcett, 1974.

Interviews

BOOK

*Milazzo, Lee, ed. *Conversations With JCO.* Jackson: U P Mississippi, 1989.

Critical Studies

BOOKS

Bastian, Katherine. *JCO's Short Stories: Between Tradition and Innovation.* Frankfurt am Main: Lang, 1983.

Bender, Eileen Teper. *JCO: Artist in Residence.* Bloomington: Indiana U P, 1987.

*Creighton, Joanne V. *JCO.* Boston: Twayne, 1979.

*Creighton. *JCO: Novels of the Middle Years.* NY: Twayne, 1992.

Friedman, Ellen G. *JCO.* NY: Ungar, 1980.

Grant, Mary Kathryn. *The Tragic Vision of JCO.* Durham, NC: Duke U P, 1978.

*Johnson, Greg. *Understanding JCO.* Columbia: U South Carolina P, 1987.

Norman, Torborg. *Isolation and Contact: A Study of Character Relation-ships in JCO's Short Stories 1963–1980.* Göteborg, Sweden: Acta Universitatis Gothoburgensis, 1984.

Waller, G F. *Dreaming America: Obsession and Transcendence in the Fiction of JCO.* Baton Rouge: Louisiana State U P, 1979.

COLLECTIONS OF ESSAYS

*Bloom, Harold, ed. *JCO.* NY: Chelsea House, 1987.

*Wagner, Linda W, ed. *Critical Essays on JCO,* preface by JCO. Boston: Hall, 1979.

BOOK SECTIONS

*Allen, Mary. "The Terrified Women of JCO." *The Necessary Blankness: Women in Major American Fiction of the Sixties* (Urbana: U Illinois P, 1976), 133–159.

Coale, Samuel Chase. "JCO: Contending Spirits." In *Hawthorne's Shadow* (Lexington: U P Kentucky, 1985), 161–179. Rpt Bloom.

Friedman, Ellen. "The Journey From the 'I' to the 'Eye': *Wonderland.*" Wagner, 102–122. Rpt Friedman.

Karl, Frederick R. *American Fictions, 1940–1980* (NY: Harper & Row, 1983), 298–302. Rpt as "Modes of Survival," Bloom.

*Kazin, Alfred. "Cassandras: Porter to O." *Bright Book of Life* (Boston: Atlantic/Little, Brown, 1973), 163–205. Excerpted as "On JCO," Wagner.

Malin, Irving. "Possessive Material." Wagner, 39–41.

Nodelman, Perry. "The Sense of Unending: JCO's *Bellefleur* as an Experi-ment in Feminine Storytelling." *Breaking the Sequence: Women's Experimental Fiction,* ed Ellen G Friedman & Miriam Fuchs (Princeton, NJ: Princeton U P, 1989), 250–264.

Showalter, Elaine. "JCO's 'The Dead' and Feminist Criticism." *Faith of a (Woman) Writer,* ed Alice Kessler-Harris & William McBrien (West-port, Conn: Greenwood, 1988), 13–19.

Stevens, Peter. "The Poetry of JCO." Wagner, 123–147.

Trachtenberg, Stanley. "Desire, Hypocrisy, and Ambition in Academe: JCO's *Hungry Ghosts.*" *The American Writer and the University,* ed Ben Siegel (Newark: U Delaware P, 1989), 39–53.

Waller, G F. "Through Obsession to Transcendence: The Lawrentian Mode in O's Recent Fiction." Wagner, 161–173.

ARTICLES

Avant, John Alfred. "*The Hungry Ghosts* by JCO." *New Republic,* 171 (31 Aug 1974), 30–31. Rpt Wagner.

Bedient, Calvin. "Vivid and Dazzling." *Nation,* 209 (1 Dec 1969), 609–611. Rpt Wagner.

Bedient. "The Story of Sleeping Beauty and a Love That Is Like Hatred." *New York Times Book Review* (14 Oct 1973), 1, 18. Rpt as "Sleeping Beauty and the Love Like Hatred," Bloom.

Bender, Eileen T. "Autonomy and Influence: JCO's *Marriages and Infidelities.*" *Soundings,* 58 (Fall 1975), 390–406. Rpt Bloom.

Burwell, Rose Marie. "The Process of Individuation as Narrative Structure: JCO's *Do With Me What You Will.*" *Critique,* 17, no 2 (1975), 93–106.

Chell, Cara. "Un-Tricking the Eye: JCO and the Feminist Ghost Story." *Arizona Quarterly,* 41 (Spring 1985), 5–23.

Coulthard, A R. "JCO's 'Where Are You Going, Where Have You Been?' as Pure Realism." *Studies in Short Fiction,* 26 (Fall 1989), 505–510.

*Creighton, Joanne V. "Unliberated Women in JCO's Fiction." *World Literature Written in English,* 17 (Apr 1978), 165–175. Rpt Wagner.

Daly, Brenda O. "An Unfilmable Conclusion: JCO at the Movies." *Journal of Popular Culture,* 23 (Winter 1989), 101–114.

*Dean, Sharon L. "Faith and Art: JCO's *Son of the Morning.*" *Critique,* 28 (Spring 1987), 135–147.

Denne, Constance Ayers. "JCO's Women." *Nation,* 219 (7 Dec 1974), 597–599.

*Ditsky, John. "The Man on the Quaker Oats Box: Characteristics of Recent Experimental Fiction." *Georgia Review,* 26 (Fall 1972), 297–313.

Early, Gerald. "The Grace of Slaughter: A Review-Essay of JCO's *On Boxing.*" *Iowa Review,* 18 (Fall 1988), 173–186.

Easterly, Joan. "The Shadow of a Satyr in O's 'Where Are You Going, Where Have You Been?'" *Studies in Short Fiction,* 27 (Fall 1990), 537–543.

Edwards, Thomas R. "The House of Atreus Now." *New York Times Book Review* (16 Aug 1981), 1, 18. Rpt Bloom.

*Fossum, Robert H. "Only Control: The Novels of JCO." *Studies in the Novel,* 7 (Summer 1975), 285–297. Rpt Wagner.

Gardner, John. "The Strange Real World." *New York Times Book Review* (20 Jul 1980), 1, 21. Rpt Bloom.

*Giles, James R. "Suffering, Transcendence, and Artistic 'Form': JCO's *them.*" *Arizona Quarterly,* 32 (Autumn 1976), 213–226.

Gillis, Christina Marsden. "'Where Are You Going, Where Have You Been?': Seduction, Space and a Fictional Mode." *Studies in Short Fiction,* 18 (Winter 1981), 65–70.

*Godwin, Gail. "An O Scrapbook." *North American Review,* 256 (Winter 1971), 67–70.

Keyser, Elizabeth Lennox. "*A Bloodsmoor Romance:* JCO's Little Women." *Women's Studies,* 14, no 3 (1988), 211–223.

Liston, William T. "Her Brother's Keeper." *Southern Humanities Review,* 11 (Spring 1977), 195–203.

*Madden, David. "*Upon the Sweeping Flood.*" *Studies in Short Fiction,* 4 (Summer 1967), 369–373. Rpt as "The Violent World of JCO." *The Poetic Image in 6 Genres* by Madden (Carbondale: Southern Illinois U P, 1969). Rpt as "*Upon the Sweeping Flood,*" Wagner.

Martin, Carol A. "Art and Myth in JCO's 'The Sacred Marriage.'" *Midwest Quarterly,* 28 (Summer 1987), 540–552.

Park, Sue Simpson. "A Study in Counterpoint: JCO's 'How I Contemplated the World From the Detroit House of Correction and Began My Life Over Again.'" *Modern Fiction Studies,* 22 (Summer 1976), 213–224.

Petite, Joseph. "'Out of the Machine': JCO and the Liberation of Woman." *Kansas Quarterly,* 9 (Spring 1977), 75–79.

Petite. "The Marriage Cycle of JCO." *Journal of Evolutionary Psychology,* 5 (Aug 1984), 223–236.

*Pickering, Samuel F, Jr. "The Short Stories of JCO." *Georgia Review,* 28 (Summer 1974), 218–226.

Pinsker, Sanford. "Suburban Molesters: JCO's *Expensive People.*" *Midwest Quarterly,* 19 (Autumn 1977), 89–103. Rpt Wagner.

Pinsker. "JCO and the New Naturalism." *Southern Review,* ns 15 (Jan 1979), 52–63.

Rozga, Margaret. "Threatening Places, Hiding Places: The Midwest in Selected Stories by JCO." *Midwest Miscellany,* 18 (1990), 34–44.

Schulz, Gretchen & R J R Rockwood. "In Fairyland, Without a Map: Connie's Exploration Inward in JCO's 'Where Are You Going, Where Have You Been?'" *Literature & Psychology,* 30, no 3–4 (1980), 155–167.

Strandberg, Victor. "Sex, Violence, and Philosophy in *You Must Remember This*." *Studies in American Fiction,* 17 (Spring 1989), 3–17.

*Sullivan, Walter. "The Artificial Demon: JCO and the Dimensions of the Real." *Hollins Critic,* 9 (Dec 1972), 1–12. Rpt Wagner, Bloom.

*Taylor, Gordon O. "JCO, Artist in *Wonderland*." *Southern Review,* ns 10 (Apr 1974), 490–503. Rpt Bloom.

*Wagner, Linda. "JCO: The Changing Shapes of Her Realities." *Great Lakes Review,* 5 (Winter 1979), 15–23. Rpt *American Modern: Essays in Fiction and Poetry* by Wagner (Port Washington, NY: Kennikat, 1980). Augmented Wagner.

Waller, G F. "JCO's *Wonderland*: An Introduction." *Dalhousie Review,* 54 (Autumn 1974), 480–490. Rpt Bloom.

Wegs, Joyce M. "'Don't You Know Who I Am?': The Grotesque in O's 'Where Are You Going, Where Have You Been?'" *Journal of Narrative Technique,* 5 (Jan 1975), 66–72. Rpt Wagner.

Weinberger, G J. "Who Is Arnold Friend? The Other Self in JCO's 'Where Are You Going, Where Have You Been?'" *American Imago,* 45 (Summer 1988), 205–215.

Wesley, Marilyn C. "The Transgressive Heroine: JCO's 'Stalking.'" *Studies in Short Fiction,* 27 (Winter 1990), 15–20.

— *Judith S. Baughman*

FLANNERY O'CONNOR

Savannah, Ga, 25 March 1925–Milledgeville, Ga, 3 Aug 1964

The earliest interest in Flannery O'Connor was based to a great extent upon the grotesque extremes of many of her characters. A more balanced understanding has come posthumously. O'Connor's readers have slowly reconciled her biting southern humor with her religious parables. Her reputation as a writer of religious themes now seems permanently assured. Her position in the history of American literature—the degree of influence from previous southern humorists, from the American romance tradition, and from continental philosophy and literature—is not yet fixed. Interest in O'Connor and her work grows steadily.

Bibliographies

*Farmer, David. *FO'C: A Descriptive Bibliography*. NY: Garland, 1981. Primary.

*Golden, Robert E & Mary C Sullivan. *FO'C and Caroline Gordon: A Reference Guide*. Boston: Hall, 1977. Secondary.

Books

Wise Blood. NY: Harcourt, Brace, 1952. Novel.

A Good Man Is Hard To Find. NY: Harcourt, Brace, 1955; *The Artificial Nigger and Other Tales*. London: Spearman, 1957. Stories.

The Violent Bear It Away. NY: Farrar, Straus & Cudahy, 1960. Novel.

Everything That Rises Must Converge. NY: Farrar, Straus & Giroux, 1965. Stories.

Mystery and Manners: Occasional Prose, ed Sally & Robert Fitzgerald. NY: Farrar, Straus & Giroux, 1969.

The Presence of Grace and Other Book Reviews, comp Leo J Zuber; ed with intro by Carter W Martin. Athens: U Georgia P, 1983.

Letters

The Habit of Being, ed Sally Fitzgerald. NY: Farrar, Straus & Giroux, 1979.

The Correspondence of FO'C and the Brainard Cheneys, ed C Ralph Stephens. Jackson: U P Mississippi, 1986.

Other

"Introduction." *A Memoir of Mary Ann* by the Dominican Nuns of Our Lady of Perpetual Help Home, Atlanta, Georgia (NY: Farrar, Straus & Cudahy, 1961), 3–21. Rpt *Mystery and Manners.*

Collections

Three by FO'C. NY: NAL, 1964 *(Wise Blood, A Good Man Is Hard To Find,* and *The Violent Bear It Away).* Rev ed, NY: NAL, 1983 *(Wise Blood, Everything That Rises Must Converge, The Violent Bear It Away).*

The Complete Stories of FO'C. NY: Farrar, Straus & Giroux, 1971.

FO'C: Collected Works, ed & annotated by Sally Fitzgerald. NY: Library of America, 1988.

Manuscripts & Archives

Georgia C Library, Milledgeville.

Biographies

BOOKS

Fickett, Harold & Douglas R Gilbert. *FO'C: Images of Grace.* Grand Rapids, Mich: Eerdmans, 1986. Biographical photo essay.

*Getz, Lorine M. *FO'C: Her Life, Library and Book Reviews.* NY: Mellen, 1980.

BOOK SECTIONS

Fitzgerald, Robert. Introduction. *Everything That Rises Must Converge,* vii–xxxiv. Excerpted Paulson.

Giroux, Robert. Introduction. *The Complete Stories of FO'C,* vii–xvii.

ARTICLES

*Abbot, Louise H. "Remembering FO'C." *Southern Literary Journal,* 2 (Spring 1970), 3–25.

Cash, Jean. "FO'C as Lecturer: '. . . A Secret Desire to Rival Charles Dickens.'" *Flannery O'Connor Bulletin,* 16 (1987), 1–15.

Fitzgerald, Sally. "A Master Class: From the Correspondence of Caroline Gordon and FO'C." *Georgia Review,* 33 (Winter 1979), 827–846.

*Lee, Maryat. "Flannery, 1957." *Flannery O'Connor Bulletin,* 5 (1976), 39–60.

*Tate, James. "An O'C Remembrance." *Flannery O'Connor Bulletin,* 17 (1988), 65–68.

*Tate, Mary Barbara. "FO'C at Home in Milledgeville." *Studies in the Literary Imagination,* 20 (Fall 1987), 31–36.

Westling, Louise. "FO'C and Rebekah Poller: A Correspondence." *Flannery O'Connor Bulletin,* 12 (1983), 68–76.

Interviews

BOOK

Magee, Rosemary, ed. *Conversations With FO'C.* Jackson: U P Mississippi, 1987.

ARTICLE

Whittier, Anthony. "The Art of Fiction XIX: FO'C." *Paris Review,* 5 (Autumn–Winter 1957), 42–64. Rpt *Writers at Work [First Series],* ed with intro by Malcolm Cowley (NY: Viking, 1958).

Critical Studies

BOOKS

*Asals, Frederick. *FO'C: The Imagination of Extremity.* Athens: U Georgia P, 1982.

Baumgaertner, Jill P. *FO'C: A Proper Scaring.* Wheaton, Ill: Shaw, 1988.

*Brinkmeyer, Robert H, Jr. *The Art & Vision of FO'C.* Baton Rouge: Louisiana State U P, 1989.

Coles, Robert. *FO'C's South*. Baton Rouge: Louisiana State U P, 1980.

Desmond, John F. *Risen Sons: FO'C's Vision of History*. Athens: U Georgia P, 1987.

Driskell, Leon & Joan T Brittain. *The Eternal Crossroads; The Art of FO'C*. Lexington: U P Kentucky, 1971.

Feeley, Sister Kathleen. *FO'C: Voice of the Peacock*. New Brunswick, NJ: Rutgers U P, 1972.

Gentry, Marshall Bruce. *FO'C's Religion of the Grotesque*. Jackson: U P Mississippi, 1986.

*Giannone, Richard. *FO'C and the Mystery of Love*. Urbana: U Illinois P, 1989.

*Grimshaw, James A, Jr. *The FO'C Companion*. Westport, Conn: Greenwood, 1981.

Kessler, Edward. *FO'C and the Language of Apocalypse*. Princeton, NJ: Princeton U P, 1986.

Kinney, Arthur F. *FO'C's Library: Resources of Being*. Athens: U Georgia P, 1985.

Martin, Carter W. *The True Country: Themes in the Fiction of FO'C*. Nashville, Tenn: Vanderbilt U P, 1968.

May, John R. *The Pruning Word: The Parables of FO'C*. Notre Dame, Ind: U Notre Dame P, 1976.

McFarland, Dorothy Tuck. *FO'C*. NY: Ungar, 1976.

Muller, Gilbert H. *Nightmares and Visions: FO'C and the Catholic Grotesque*. Athens: U Georgia P, 1972.

Orvell, Miles. *Invisible Parade: The Fiction of FO'C*. Philadelphia: Temple U P, 1972.

*Paulson, Suzanne Morrow. *FO'C: A Study of the Short Fiction*. Boston: Twayne, 1988. Includes excerpts from other critics, pp. 151–223.

*Stephens, Martha. *The Question of FO'C*. Baton Rouge: Louisiana State U P, 1973.

*Walters, Dorothy. *FO'C*. NY: Twayne, 1973.

Westling, Louise. *Sacred Groves and Ravaged Gardens: The Fiction of Eudora Welty, Carson McCullers, and FO'C*. Athens: U Georgia P, 1985.

COLLECTIONS OF ESSAYS

*Bloom, Harold, ed. *FO'C*. NY: Chelsea House, 1986.

*Friedman, Melvin J & Beverly Lyon Clark, eds. *Critical Essays on FO'C*. Boston: Hall, 1985.

*Friedman & Lewis A Lawson, eds. *The Added Dimension: The Art and Mind of FO'C.* NY: Fordham U P, rev 1977.

Westarp, Karl–Heinz & Jan Nordby Gretlund, eds. *Realist of Distances: FO'C Revisited.* Aarhus, Denmark: Aarhus U P, 1987.

SPECIAL JOURNALS

Critique, 2 (Fall 1958). FO'C/J F Powers issue.

Esprit, 8 (Winter 1964). FO'C issue.

*Flannery O'Connor Bulletin (annually, 1972–).

*Flannery O'Connor Bulletin Index (1972–1986).

Renascence, 22 (Autumn 1969). FO'C issue.

Studies in the Literary Imagination, 20 (Fall 1987). FO'C issue.

BOOK SECTIONS

Ashley, Jack Dillard. "Throwing the Big Book: The Narrator Voice in FO'C's Stories." Westarp & Gretlund, 73–81.

Brown, Ashley. "FO'C: A Literary Memoir." Westarp & Gretlund, 18–29.

Gretlund, Jan Nordby. "The Side of the Road: FO'C's Social Sensibility." Westarp & Gretlund, 197–207.

Ireland, Patrick J. "The Sacred and the Profane: Redefining FO'C's Vision." Westarp & Gretlund, 186–196.

*Lawson, Lewis A. "*Wise Blood* and the Grotesque." *Another Generation* (Jackson: U P Mississippi, 1984), 22–37.

Malin, Irving. *New American Gothic* (Carbondale: Southern Illinois U P, 1962), passim.

*Walker, Alice. "Beyond the Peacock: The Reconstruction of FO'C." *In Search of Our Mothers' Gardens* (San Diego: Harcourt Brace Jovanovich, 1983), 71–81. Rpt Friedman & Clark.

ARTICLES

Allen, William R. "The Cage of Matter: The World as Zoo in FO'C's *Wise Blood.*" *American Literature,* 58 (May 1986), 256–270.

Asals, Frederick. "Hawthorne, Mary Ann, and 'The Lame Shall Enter First.'" *Flannery O'Connor Bulletin,* 2 (1973), 3–18.

*Asals. "FO'C as Novelist: A Defense." *Flannery O'Connor Bulletin,* 3 (1974), 23–39.

Asals. "The Double in FO'C's Stories." *Flannery O'Connor Bulletin,* 9 (1980), 49–86. Rev & rpt Asals, Bloom.

Brinkmeyer, Robert H, Jr. "A Closer Walk With Thee: FO'C and Southern Fundamentalists." *Southern Literary Journal,* 18 (Spring 1986), 3–13.

Browning, Preston M, Jr. "FO'C and the Demonic." *Modern Fiction Studies,* 19 (Spring 1973), 29–41.

Burke, William M. "Protagonists and Antagonists in the Fiction of FO'C." *Southern Literary Journal,* 20 (Spring 1988), 99–111.

Burns, Shannon. "The Literary Theory of FO'C and Nathaniel Hawthorne." *Flannery O'Connor Bulletin,* 7 (Autumn 1978), 101–113.

Burns, Stuart L. "FO'C's Literary Apprenticeship." *Renascence,* 22 (Aug 1969), 3–16.

*Burns. "Freaks in a Circus Tent: FO'C's Christ-Haunted Characters." *Flannery O'Connor Bulletin,* 1 (1972), 2–23.

Carlson, Thomas M. "FO'C: The Manichaean Dilemma." *Sewanee Review,* 77 (Apr–Jun 1969), 254–276.

Cheney, Brainard. "Miss O'C Creates Unusual Humor Out of Ordinary Sin." *Sewanee Review,* 71 (Oct–Dec 1963), 644–652.

Coulthard, A R. "From Sermon to Parable: Four Conversion Stories by FO'C." *American Literature,* 55 (Mar 1983), 55–71.

Desmond, John F. "FO'C's Sense of Place." *Southern Humanities Review,* 10 (Summer 1976), 251–259.

Doxey, William S. "A Dissenting Opinion of FO'C's 'A Good Man Is Hard To Find.'" *Studies in Short Fiction,* 10 (Spring 1973), 199–204.

*Drake, Robert. "FO'C and American Literature." *Flannery O'Connor Bulletin,* 3 (1974), 1–22.

Edelstein, Mark G. "FO'C and the Problem of Modern Satire." *Studies in Short Fiction,* 12 (Spring 1975), 139–144.

*Emerick, Ronald. "Hawthorne and O'C: A Literary Kinship." *Flannery O'Connor Bulletin,* 18 (1989), 46–54.

Fitzgerald, Robert. "The Countryside and the True Country." *Sewanee Review,* 70 (Jul–Sep 1962), 380–394. Rpt Bloom.

Giannone, Richard. "'The Artificial Nigger' and the Redemptive Quality of Suffering." *Flannery O'Connor Bulletin,* 12 (1983), 4–16.

Gordon, Caroline. "Heresy in Dixie." *Sewanee Review,* 76 (Apr–Jun 1968), 263-297.

*Gordon, Sarah. "FO'C and the Common Reader." *Flannery O'Connor Bulletin,* 10 (1981), 38–45. Excerpted Paulson.

*Hawkes, John. "FO'C's Devil." *Sewanee Review*, 70 (Jul–Sep 1962), 395–407. Rpt Friedman & Clark, Bloom.

Kahane, Claire. "The Artificial Niggers." *Massachusetts Review*, 19 (Spring 1978), 183–198.

Kane, Richard. "Positive Destruction in the Fiction of FO'C." *Southern Literary Journal*, 20 (Fall 1987), 45–60.

*Katz, Claire. "FO'C's Rage of Vision." *American Literature*, 46 (Mar 1974), 54–67. Rpt as by Claire Kahane, Friedman & Clark. Excerpted as by Claire Katz [Kahane], Paulson.

Klug, M A. "FO'C and the Manichaean Spirit of Modernism." *Southern Humanities Review*, 17 (Fall 1983), 303–314. Excerpted Paulson.

Koon, William. "'Hep Me Not To Be So Mean': FO'C's Subjectivity." *Southern Review*, 15 (Apr 1979), 322–332.

*Lawson, Lewis A. "FO'C and the Grotesque: *Wise Blood*." *Renascence*, 17 (Spring 1965), 137–147, 156. Rpt as "The Perfect Deformity: *Wise Blood*," Bloom.

Linehan, Thomas M. "Anagogical Realism in FO'C." *Renascence*, 37 (Winter 1985), 80–95.

MacDonald, Russ. "Comedy and FO'C." *South Atlantic Quarterly*, 81 (Spring 1982), 188–201.

Magistrale, Tony. "'I'm Alien to a Great Deal': FO'C and the Modernist Ethic." *Journal of American Studies*, 24 (Apr 1990), 93–98.

Martin, Carter W. "Comedy and Humor in FO'C's Fiction." *Flannery O'Connor Bulletin*, 4 (1975), 1–12.

May, John R. "The Methodological Limits of FO'C's Critics." *Flannery O'Connor Bulletin*, 15 (1986), 16–28.

*Morton, Mary L. "Doubling in FO'C's Female Characters: Animus and Animal." *Southern Quarterly*, 23 (Summer 1985), 57–63. Excerpted Paulson.

Nichols, Loxley F. "FO'C's 'Intellectual Vaudeville': Masks of Mother and Daughter." *Studies in the Literary Imagination*, 20 (Fall 1987), 15–29.

Nisly, Paul W. "The Prison of the Self: Isolation in FO'C's Fiction." *Studies in Short Fiction*, 17 (Winter 1980), 49–54.

Nisly. "The Mystery of Evil: FO'C's Gothic Power." *Flannery O'Connor Bulletin*, 11 (1982), 25–35.

*Oates, Joyce Carol. "The Visionary Art of FO'C." *Southern Humanities Review*, 7 (Summer 1973), 235–246. Rpt *Fiction by American Women*, ed Winifred F Bevilacqua (Port Washington, NY: Associated Faculty P, 1983). Rpt Bloom.

Oreovicz, Cheryl Z. "Seduced by Language: The Case of Joy-Hulga Hopewell." *Studies in American Fiction,* 7 (Autumn 1979), 221–228.

Park, Clara C. "Crippled Laughter: Toward Understanding FO'C." *American Scholar,* 51 (Spring 1982), 249–257.

*Petry, Alice Hall. "Miss O'C and Mrs. Mitchell: The Example of 'Everything That Rises.'" *Southern Quarterly,* 27 (Summer 1989), 5–15.

Rubin, Louis D, Jr. "FO'C's Company of Southerners: or, 'The Artificial Nigger' Read as Fiction Rather Than Theology." *Flannery O'Connor Bulletin,* 6 (1977), 47–71. Rpt *A Gallery of Southerners* by Rubin (Baton Rouge: Louisiana State U P, 1982).

Russell, Shannon. "Space and the Movement Through Space in *Everything That Rises Must Converge:* A Consideration of FO'C's Imaginative Vision." *Southern Literary Journal,* 20 (Spring 1988), 81–98.

Satterfield, Ben. "*Wise Blood,* Artistic Anemia, and the Hemorrhaging of O'C Criticism." *Studies in American Fiction,* 17 (Spring 1989), 33–50.

Schleifer, Ronald. "Rural Gothic: The Stories of FO'C." *Modern Fiction Studies,* 28 (Aug 1982), 475–485. Rpt Friedman & Clark, Bloom.

Spivey, Ted R. "FO'C, James Joyce, and the City." *Studies in the Literary Imagination,* 20 (Fall 1987), 87–96.

*Stephens, Martha. "FO'C and the Sanctified Sinner Tradition." *Arizona Quarterly,* 24 (Autumn 1968), 223–239.

Tate, James O, Jr. "FO'C's Counterplot." *Southern Review,* 16 (Oct 1980), 869–878.

Tedford, Barbara W. "FO'C and the Social Classes." *Southern Literary Journal,* 13 (Spring 1981), 27–40.

Thorp, Willard. "Suggs and Sut in Modern Dress: The Latest Chapter in Southern Humor." *Mississippi Quarterly,* 13 (Fall 1960), 169–175.

*Wray, Virginia F. "FO'C in the American Romance Tradition." *Flannery O'Connor Bulletin,* 6 (1977), 83–98.

Young, Thomas D. "FO'C's View of the South: God's Earth and His Universe." *Studies in the Literary Imagination,* 20 (Fall 1987), 5–14.

— *David H. Payne*

KATHERINE ANNE PORTER

Indian Creek, Tex, 15 May 1890–Silver Spring, Md, 18 Sep 1980

Katherine Anne Porter won critical praise with the appearance in 1930 of her first collection of stories, *Flowering Judas;* but not until the publication in 1962 of her novel *Ship of Fools* did she acquire a large popular audience. In 1966 her collected short fiction won both the Pulitzer Prize and the National Book Award. Praised for her craftsmanship and style, Porter preferred to stand with the traditionalists. The themes that dominate her fiction include self-betrayal and disillusionment, the unintentional collusion with evil, and the arduous journey to truth, obscured by false ideals and the mistaking of external order for spiritual meaning.

Bibliography

*Hilt, Kathryn & Ruth M Alvarez. *KAP: An Annotated Bibliography.* NY: Garland, 1990. Primary & secondary.

Books

My *Chinese Marriage* by May Taim Franking. NY: Duffield, 1921. Ghost-written by KAP. Nonfiction.

Outline of Mexican Popular Arts and Crafts. Los Angeles: Young & McCallister, 1922. Nonfiction.

Flowering Judas. NY: Harcourt, Brace, 1930. Augmented as *Flowering Judas and Other Stories.* NY: Harcourt, Brace, 1935; *Flowering Judas.* London: Cape, 1936.

Hacienda. NY: Harrison of Paris, 1934. Novella.

Noon Wine. Detroit: Schuman, 1937. Novella.

Pale Horse, Pale Rider: Three Short Novels. NY: Harcourt, Brace, 1939.

The Leaning Tower and Other Stories. NY: Harcourt, Brace, 1944.

The Days Before. NY: Harcourt, Brace, 1952. Essays, letters & speeches.

A Defense of Circe. NY: Harcourt, Brace, 1954. Nonfiction.

The Old Order: Stories of the South. NY: Harcourt, Brace, 1955.

Ship of Fools. Boston & Toronto: Atlantic/Little, Brown, 1962. Novel.

The Collected Stories of KAP. London: Cape, 1964. Augmented ed, NY: Harcourt, Brace & World, 1965.

A Christmas Story. NY: Delacorte, 1967. Nonfiction.

The Collected Essays and Occasional Writings of KAP. NY: Lawrence/Delacorte, 1970.

The Never-Ending Wrong. Boston & Toronto: Atlantic/Little, Brown, 1977. Nonfiction.

"This Strange, Old World" and Other Book Reviews by KAP, ed Darlene Harbour Unrue. Athens: U Georgia P, 1991.

Letters

Letters of KAP, ed Isabel Bayley. NY: Atlantic Monthly, 1990.

Other

"Introduction." *What Price Marriage?* (NY: Sears, 1927), 7–13. Compilation of essays with intro by KAP signed "Hamblen Sears."

KAP's French Song-Book. Npl: Harrison of Paris, nd. Translations.

"Introduction." *A Curtain of Green* by Eudora Welty (Garden City, NY: Doubleday, Doran, 1941), xi–xxiii.

The Itching Parrot by José Joaquín Fernández de Lizardi; trans with intro by KAP. Garden City, NY: Doubleday, Doran, 1942. Novel.

"Introduction." *Fiesta in November,* ed Angel Flores & Dudley Poore (Boston: Houghton Mifflin, 1942),1–10.

Manuscripts & Archives

U of Maryland, College Park, Library.

Biographies

BOOKS

Givner, Joan. *KAP: A Life.* NY: Simon & Schuster, 1982.

Lopez, Enrique Hank. *Conversations With KAP: Refugee From Indian Creek.* Boston: Little, Brown, 1981.

ARTICLE

Liberman, M M. "Meeting Miss P." *Georgia Review,* 41 (Summer 1987), 299–303.

Interviews

BOOK

*Givner, Joan, ed. *KAP: Conversations.* Jackson: U P Mississippi, 1987.

BOOK SECTIONS

"Alice in Wonderland," with KAP, Bertrand Russell & Mark Van Doren. *The New Invitation to Learning,* ed Van Doren (NY: Random House, 1942), 208–220.

"Moll Flanders," with KAP, Huntington Cairns, Allen Tate & Mark Van Doren. *The Invitation to Learning,* ed Cairns, Tate & Van Doren (NY: Random House, 1941), 137–151.

"Tom Jones," with KAP, Allen Tate & Mark Van Doren. *The New Invitation to Learning,* ed Van Doren (NY: Random House, 1942), 194–205.

"The Turn of the Screw," with KAP, Allen Tate & Mark Van Doren. *The New Invitation to Learning,* ed Van Doren (NY: Random House, 1942), 223–235. Rpt Givner (1987).

ARTICLES

Allen, Henry. "A Lioness of Literature Looks Back." *Los Angeles Times Calendar* (7 Jul 1974), 1, 64–65.

Dorsey, John. "KAP. . . ." *Baltimore Sun Magazine* (26 Oct 1969), 16, 18–19, 21, 23, 40–41. Rpt Givner (1987).

Lopez, Hank. "A Country and Some People I Love." *Harper's,* 231 (Sep 1965), 58–62, 65–68. Rpt Warren, Givner (1987).

Newquist, Roy. "An Interview With KAP." *McCall's,* 92 (Aug 1965), 88–89, 137–143. Rpt Givner (1987).

"An *Open Mind* Profile: KAP Talks With Glenway Wescott and Eric F Goldman." *Georgia Review,* 41 (Winter 1987), 769–795.

*"Recent Southern Fiction: A Panel Discussion," with KAP, Flannery O'Connor, Caroline Gordon, Madison Jones & Louis D Rubin, Jr. *Bulletin of Wesleyan College*, 41 (Jan 1961), 1–16. Rpt Givner (1987).

*Thompson, Barbara. "The Art of Fiction XXIX: KAP." *Paris Review*, 8 (Winter–Spring 1963), 87–114. Rpt *Writers at Work, Second Series*, ed George Plimpton (NY: Viking, 1963). Rpt Hartley & Core, Givner (1987).

Critical Studies

BOOKS

DeMouy, Jane Krouse. *KAP's Women: The Eye of Her Fiction*. Austin: U Texas P, 1983.

*Hardy, John Edward. *KAP*. NY: Ungar, 1973.

*Hendrick, Willene & George. *KAP*. Boston: Twayne, rev 1988.

Liberman, M M. *KAP's Fiction*. Detroit, Mich: Wayne State U P, 1971.

Mooney, Harry John, Jr. *The Fiction and Criticism of KAP*. Pittsburgh, Pa: U Pittsburgh P, rev 1962.

Nance, William L. *KAP & the Art of Rejection*. Chapel Hill: U North Carolina P, 1964.

Unrue, Darlene Harbour. *Truth and Vision in KAP's Fiction*. Athens: U Georgia P, 1985.

*Unrue. *Understanding KAP*. Columbia: U South Carolina P, 1988.

*Walsh, Thomas F. *KAP and Mexico: The Illusion of Eden*. Austin: U Texas P, 1992.

West, Ray B, Jr. *KAP*. Minneapolis: U Minnesota P, 1963.

COLLECTIONS OF ESSAYS

Bloom, Harold, ed. *KAP*. NY: Chelsea House, 1986.

*Hartley, Lodwick & George Core, eds. *KAP: A Critical Symposium*. Athens: U Georgia P, 1969.

Machann, Clinton & William Bedford Clark, eds. *KAP and Texas: An Uneasy Relationship*. College Station: Texas A&M U P, 1990.

Warren, Robert Penn, ed. *KAP: A Collection of Critical Essays*. Englewood Cliffs, NJ: Prentice-Hall, 1979.

SPECIAL JOURNAL

Four Quarters, 12 (Nov 1962). KAP issue.

BOOK SECTIONS

Auchincloss, Louis. "KAP." *Pioneers & Caretakers* (Minneapolis: U Minnesota P, 1965), 136–151.

Joselyn, Sister M. "Animal Imagery in KAP's Fiction." *Myth and Symbol,* ed Bernice Slote (Lincoln: U Nebraska P, 1963), 101–115.

Stout, Janis P. "KAP and the Reticent Style." *Strategies of Reticence: Silence and Meaning in the Works of Jane Austen, Willa Cather, KAP, and Joan Didion* (Charlottesville: U P Virginia, 1990), 112–146.

Wescott, Glenway. "KAP Personally." *Images of Truth* (NY: Harper & Row, 1962), 25–58. Rpt Hartley & Core, Warren.

ARTICLES

*Brooks, Cleanth. "On 'The Grave.'" *Yale Review,* 55 (Dec 1966), 275–279.

Core, George. "The *Best* Residuum of Truth." *Georgia Review,* 20 (Fall 1966), 278–291. Augmented as "'Holiday': A Vision of Pastoral," Hartley & Core.

Curley, Daniel. "Treasure in 'The Grave.'" *Modern Fiction Studies,* 9 (Winter 1963–1964), 377–384.

Gottfried, Leon. "Death's Other Kingdom: Dantesque and Theological Symbolism in 'Flowering Judas.'" *PMLA,* 84 (Jan 1969), 112–124.

Hartley, Lodwick. "Dark Voyagers: A Study of KAP's *Ship of Fools.*" *University Review,* 30 (Winter 1963), 83–94.

*Heilman, Robert B. "*Ship of Fools:* Notes on Style." *Four Quarters,* 12 (Nov 1962), 46–55. Rpt Hartley & Core, Bloom.

Hertz, Robert N. "Sebastian Brant and P's *Ship of Fools.*" *Midwest Quarterly,* 6 (Jul 1965), 389–401.

Johnson, James William. "Another Look at KAP." *Virginia Quarterly Review,* 36 (Autumn 1960), 598–613. Rpt Hartley & Core.

Kirkpatrick, Smith. "*Ship of Fools.*" *Sewanee Review,* 71 (Jan–Mar 1963), 94–98. Rpt Warren.

Liberman, M M. "The Responsibility of the Novelist: The Critical Reception of *Ship of Fools.*" *Criticism,* 8 (Fall 1966), 377–388.

Perry, Robert L. "P's 'Hacienda' and the Theme of Change." *Midwest Quarterly*, 6 (Jul 1965), 403–415.

Praeger, Leonard. "Getting and Spending: P's 'Theft.'" *Perspective*, 11 (Winter 1960), 230–234.

Ryan, Marjorie. "*Dubliners* and the Stories of KAP." *American Literature*, 31 (Jan 1960), 464–473.

Schwartz, Edward G. "The Way of Dissent: KAP's Critical Position." *Western Humanities Review*, 8 (Spring 1954), 119–130. Rpt Hartley & Core, Warren.

*Schwartz. "The Fictions of Memory." *Southwest Review*, 45 (Summer 1960), 204–215.

Stein, William Bysshe. "'Theft': P's Politics of Modern Love." *Perspective*, 11 (Winter 1960), 223–228.

Stout, Janis P. "Miranda's Guarded Speech: P and the Problem of Truth-Telling." *Philological Quarterly*, 66 (Spring 1987), 259–278.

Walsh, Thomas F. "The 'Noon Wine' Devils." *Georgia Review*, 22 (Spring 1968), 90–96.

Walsh. "Deep Similarities in 'Noon Wine.'" *Mosaic*, 9 (Fall 1975), 83–91.

*Walsh. "The Dreams Self in 'Pale Horse, Pale Rider.'" *Wascana Review*, 14 (Fall 1979), 61–79. Rpt Bloom.

Walsh. "Miranda's Ghost in 'Old Mortality.'" *College Literature*, 6 (Winter 1979–1980), 57–63.

*Warren, Robert Penn. "KAP (Irony With a Center)." *Kenyon Review*, 4 (Winter 1942), 29–42. Rpt Hartley & Core, Warren, Bloom.

Welty, Eudora. "The Eye of the Story." *Yale Review*, 55 (Dec 1965), 265–274. Rpt Hartley & Core, Warren, Bloom.

*Wiesenfarth, Brother Joseph. "Illusion and Allusion: Reflections in 'The Cracked Looking-Glass.'" *Four Quarters*, 12 (Nov 1962), 30–37. Rpt Hartley & Core.

Wiesenfarth. "Internal Opposition in P's 'Granny Weatherall.'" *Critique*, 11, no 2 (1969), 47–55.

Wiesenfarth. "The Structure of KAP's 'Theft.'" *Cithara*, 10 (May 1971), 65–71.

*Youngblood, Sarah. "Structure and Imagery in KAP's 'Pale Horse, Pale Rider.'" *Modern Fiction Studies*, 5 (Winter 1959–1960), 344–352.

— *Darlene Harbour Unrue*

GERTRUDE STEIN

Allegheny, Pa, 3 Feb 1874–Neuilly-sur-Seine, France, 27 Jul 1946

Gertrude Stein's reputation rests as much on her unconventional lifestyle and influential personality during the expatriate period as on her innovative writing. She encouraged the group of young American and British writers who had moved to Paris after World War I. With the 1909 publication of *Three Lives,* Stein anticipated the modernist period. Her writing is best known for its fusion of genres, its experimental use of language with insistent repetition and rhythm, and its unique treatment of time (a technique she called the "continuous present"). Because her writing emphasizes fragmentation, abstraction, and flux, her literary reputation has increased with the development of postmodernism, which shares a similar vision.

Bibliographies

"An Annotated Bibliography of Selected Criticism." Kellner, 311–327.

*Liston, Maureen R. *GS: An Annotated Critical Bibliography.* Kent, Ohio: Kent State U P, 1979. Secondary.

White, Ray Lewis. *GS and Alice B. Toklas: A Reference Guide.* Boston: Hall, 1984. Secondary.

*Wilson, Robert A. *GS: A Bibliography.* NY: Phoenix Bookshop, 1974. Primary & secondary.

Books

Three Lives: Stories of the Good Anna, Melanctha and the Gentle Lena. NY: Grafton, 1909.

Portrait of Mabel Dodge at the Villa Curonia. Florence: Galileiana, 1913.

Tender Buttons: Objects, Food, Rooms. NY: Claire Marie, 1914. Poems.

Have They Attacked Mary. He Giggled. West Chester, Pa: Temple, 1917.

Geography and Plays. Boston: Four Seas, 1922.

The Making of Americans: Being a History of a Family's Progress. Paris: Contact Editions/Three Mountains, 1925; NY: Boni, 1926.

Composition as Explanation. London: Hogarth, 1926. Lecture.

A Book Concluding With As a Wife Has a Cow: A Love Story. Paris: Editions de la Galerie Simon, 1926; Barton, Vt & c: Something Else, 1973.

Useful Knowledge. NY: Payson & Clarke, 1928.

A Village, Are You Ready Not Yet: A Play in Four Acts. Paris: Editions de la Galerie Simon, 1928.

An Acquaintance With Description, London: Seizin, 1929.

Lucy Church Amiably. Paris: Plain Edition, 1930; NY: Something Else, 1969.

Dix Portraits, with translations by Georges Hugnet & Virgil Thomson; illustrated by Pablo Picasso, Pavel Tchelitchew, Eugene Berard & Kristians Tonny. Paris: Editions de la Montagne, 1930.

Before the Flowers of Friendship Faded, Friendship Faded, Written on a Poem by Georges Hugnet. Paris: Plain Edition, 1931.

How to Write. Paris: Plain Edition, 1931; Barton, Vt: Something Else, 1973. Nonfiction.

Operas and Plays. Paris: Plain Edition, 1932; *Operas & Plays.* Barrytown, NY: Station Hill, 1987.

Matisse Picasso and GS With Two Shorter Stories. Paris: Plain Edition, 1933; Barton, Vt & c: Something Else, 1972.

The Autobiography of Alice B. Toklas. NY: Harcourt, Brace, 1933.

Four Saints in Three Acts: An Opera to Be Sung, intro by Carl Van Vechten. NY: Random House, 1934.

Portraits and Prayers. NY: Random House, 1934.

Lectures in America. NY: Random House, 1935.

Narration: Four Lectures, intro by Thornton Wilder. Chicago: U Chicago P, 1935.

The Geographical History of America or The Relation of Human Nature to the Human Mind, intro by Wilder. NY: Random House, 1936.

Everybody's Autobiography. NY: Random House, 1937.

Picasso. Paris & London: Batsford, 1938; NY: Scribners, 1939.

The World Is Round. NY: Scott, 1939.

Paris France. NY: Scribners, 1940.

What Are Masterpieces, foreword by Robert Bartlett Haas. Los Angeles: Conference, 1940.

Ida: A Novel. NY: Random House, 1941.

Wars I Have Seen. NY: Random House, 1945. Augmented ed, London: Batsford, 1945. Memoir.

The GS First Reader & Three Plays. Dublin & London: Fridberg, 1946; Boston: Houghton Mifflin, 1948.

Brewsie and Willie. NY: Random House, 1946.

In Savoy or Yes Is for a Very Young Man (A Play of the Resistance in France). London: Pushkin, 1946.

Four in America, intro by Wilder; preface by Donald Gallup. New Haven, Conn: Yale U P, 1947.

The Mother of Us All, with Virgil Thomson. NY: Music, 1947.

Blood on the Dining-Room Floor, foreword by Gallup. Pawlet, Vt: Banyan, 1948; with intro by Janet Hobhouse, London: Virago, 1985.

Last Operas and Plays, ed with intro by Van Vechten. NY & Toronto: Rinehart, 1949.

Things as They Are. Pawlet, Vt: Banyan, 1950.

Two: GS and Her Brother and Other Early Portraits [1908–12], foreword by Janet Flanner; note by Van Vechten. New Haven, Conn: Yale U P/ London: Cumberlege, Oxford U P, 1951.

In a Garden: An Opera in One Act, with Meyer Kupferman. NY: Mercury Music, 1951.

Mrs. Reynolds and Five Earlier Novelettes, foreword by Lloyd Frankenberg. New Haven, Conn: Yale U P / London: Cumberlege, Oxford U P, 1952.

Bee Time Vine and Other Pieces [1913–1927], preface & notes by Thomson. New Haven, Conn: Yale U P / London: Cumberlege, Oxford U P, 1953.

As Fine as Melanctha (1914–1930), foreword by Natalie Clifford Barney. New Haven, Conn: Yale U P/London: Cumberlege, Oxford U P, 1954.

Painted Lace and Other Pieces [1914–1937], intro by Daniel-Henry Kahnweiler; trans Gallup. New Haven, Conn: Yale U P / London: Cumberlege, Oxford U P, 1955.

Stanzas in Meditation and Other Poems [1929–1933], preface by Donald Sutherland. New Haven, Conn: Yale U P / London: Cumberlege, Oxford U P, 1956.

Alphabets & Birthdays, intro by Gallup. New Haven, Conn: Yale U P / London: Oxford U P, 1957.

A Novel of Thank You, intro by Van Vechten. New Haven, Conn: Yale U P, 1958.

Lucretia Borgia: A Play. NY: Albondocani, 1968.

Motor Automatism, with Leon M Solomons. NY: Phoenix Book Shop, 1969.

Fernhurst, Q.E.D., and Other Early Writings, intro by Leon Katz; note by Gallup. NY. Liveright, 1971.

Money. Los Angeles: Black Sparrow, 1973.

Reflection on the Atomic Bomb, ed with preface by Haas. Los Angeles: Black Sparrow, 1973.

How Writing Is Written, ed with preface by Haas. Los Angeles: Black Sparrow, 1974.

Letters

Sherwood Anderson/GS: Correspondence and Personal Essays, ed Ray Lewis White. Chapel Hill: U North Carolina P, 1972.

Dear Sammy: Letters From GS and Alice B. Toklas, ed with memoir by Samuel M Steward. Boston: Houghton Mifflin, 1977.

The Letters of GS and Carl Van Vechten, 1913–1946, 2 vols, ed with intro by Edward Burns. NY: Columbia U P, 1986.

Collections

Selected Writings of GS, ed with intro by Carl Van Vechten. NY: Random House, 1946.

Writings and Lectures, 1911–1945, ed Patricia Meyerowitz; intro by Elizabeth Sprigge. London: Owen, 1967. Repub as *Look at Me Now and Here I Am: Writings and Lectures, 1909–1945.* Harmondsworth, UK: Penguin, 1971.

Selected Operas and Plays, ed with intro by John Malcolm Brinnin. Pittsburgh, Pa: U Pittsburgh P, 1970.

GS on Picasso, ed Edward Burns; afterword by Leon Katz & Burns. NY: Liveright in cooperation with MOMA, 1970.

A Primer for the Gradual Understanding of GS, ed Robert Bartlett Haas. Los Angeles: Black Sparrow, 1971.

The Yale GS, ed with intro by Richard Kostelanetz. New Haven, Conn & London: Yale U P, 1980.

Really Reading GS: A Selected Anthology, ed with essays by Judy Grahn. Freedom, Calif: Crossing, 1989.

Manuscripts & Archives

Beinecke Library, Yale U.

Biographies

BOOKS

*Brinnin, John Malcolm. *The Third Rose: GS and Her World.* Boston: Little, Brown, 1959.

Gallup, Donald, ed. *The Flowers of Friendship: Letters Written to GS.* NY: Knopf, 1953.

*Mellow, James R. *Charmed Circle: GS and Company.* NY: Praeger, 1974.

Rather, Lois. *GS and California.* Oakland, Calif: Rather, 1974.

Rogers, W G. *When This You See Remember Me: GS in Person.* NY: Rinehart, 1948.

*Simon, Linda. *The Biography of Alice B. Toklas.* Garden City, NY: Doubleday, 1977.

Stavitsky, Gail. *GS: The American Connection.* NY: Deutsch Gallery, 1990.

Toklas, Alice B. *The Alice B. Toklas Cookbook.* NY: Harper, 1954.

*Toklas. *What Is Remembered.* NY: Holt, Rinehart & Winston, 1963.

Toklas. *Staying on Alone: Letters of Alice B. Toklas,* ed Edward Burns; intro by Gilbert A Harrison. NY: Liveright, 1973.

BOOK SECTIONS

Hemingway, Ernest. "Miss S Instructs," "'Une Génération Perdue,'" "A Strange Enough Ending." *A Moveable Feast* (NY: Scribners, 1964), 9–21, 23–31, 115–119.

McAlmon, Robert, with chapters by Kay Boyle. *Being Geniuses Together: 1920–1930* (Garden City, NY: Doubleday, 1968), passim.

*Stein, Leo. *Appreciation: Painting, Poetry and Prose* (NY: Crown, 1947), passim.

*Stein. *Journey into the Self,* ed Edmund Fuller (NY: Crown, 1950), passim.

*Thomson, Virgil. "A Portrait of GS," "G and the Young French Poet." *Virgil Thomson* (NY: Knopf, 1966), 169–197, passim.

Critical Studies

BOOKS

Berry, Ellen E. *Curved Thought and Textual Wandering: GS's Postmodernism.* Ann Arbor: U Michigan P, 1992.

Bowers, Jane Palatini. *"They Watch Me as They Watch This": GS's Metadrama.* Philadelphia: U Pennsylvania P, 1991.

*Bridgman, Richard. *GS in Pieces.* NY: Oxford U P, 1970.

Bush, Clive. *Halfway to Revolution: Investigation and Crisis in the Work of Henry Adams, William James and GS.* New Haven, Conn: Yale U P, 1991.

Chessman, Harriet Scott. *The Public Is Invited to Dance: Representation, the Body, and Dialogue in GS.* Stanford, Calif: Stanford U P, 1989.

Copeland, Carolyn Faunce. *Language & Time & GS.* Iowa City: U Iowa P, 1975.

*DeKoven, Marianne. *A Different Language: GS's Experimental Writing.* Madison: U Wisconsin P, 1983.

*Doane, Janice L. *Silence and Narrative: The Early Novels of GS.* Westport, Conn: Greenwood, 1986.

Dubnick, Randa. *The Structure of Obscurity: GS, Language, and Cubism.* Urbana: U Illinois P, 1984.

Fifer, Elizabeth. *Rescued Readings: A Reconstruction of GS's Difficult Texts.* Detroit, Mich: Wayne State U P, 1992.

Hoffman, Michael J. *The Development of Abstractionism in the Writings of GS.* Philadelphia: U Pennsylvania P, 1965.

*Hoffman. *GS.* NY: Twayne, 1976.

Knapp, Bettina. *GS.* NY: Continuum, 1990.

Liston, Maureen Ruth. *An Essay to Introduce GS's A Novel of Thank You.* Essen, Germany: Blaue Eule, 1987.

Maubrey-Rose, Victoria. *The Anti-Representational Response: GS's Lucy Church Amiably.* Uppsala, Sweden: Almqvist & Wiksell, 1985.

Miller, Rosalind S. *GS: Form and Intelligibility: Containing the Radcliffe Themes.* NY: Exposition, 1949.

Neumann, S C. *GS: Autobiography and the Problem of Narration*. Victoria, BC: English Literary Studies, 1979.

Reid, B L. *Art by Subtraction: A Dissenting Opinion of GS*. Norman: U Oklahoma P, 1958.

Ruddick, Lisa. *Reading GS: Body, Text, Gnosis*. Ithaca, NY: Cornell U P, 1990.

Ryan, Betsy Alayne. *GS's Theatre of the Absolute*. Ann Arbor, Mich: UMI, 1984.

Steiner, Wendy. *Exact Resemblance to Exact Resemblance: The Literary Portraiture of GS*. New Haven, Conn: Yale U P, 1978.

*Sutherland, Donald. *GS: A Biography of Her Work*. New Haven, Conn: Yale U P / London: Cumberlege, Oxford U P, 1951.

*Walker, Jayne L. *The Making of a Modernist: GS From Three Lives to Tender Buttons*. Amherst: U Massachusetts P, 1984.

Weinstein, Norman. *GS and the Literature of the Modern Consciousness*. NY: Ungar, 1970.

COLLECTIONS OF ESSAYS

Bloom, Harold, ed. *GS*. NY: Chelsea House, 1986.

Gordon, Irene, ed. *Four Americans in Paris: The Collections of GS and Her Family*. NY: Museum of Modern Art, 1970.

*Hoffman, Michael J, ed. *Critical Essays on GS*. Boston: Hall, 1986.

*Kellner, Bruce, ed. *A GS Companion: Content With the Example*. NY: Greenwood, 1988.

Kostelanetz, Richard, ed. *GS Advanced: An Anthology of Criticism*. Jefferson, NC: McFarland, 1990.

*Neuman, Shirley & Ira B Nadel, eds. *GS and the Making of Literature*. Boston: Northeastern U P, 1988.

SPECIAL JOURNALS

Lost Generation Journal, 2 (Winter 1974). GS issue.

transition, supplement (Feb 1935). GS issue.

Twentieth Century Literature, 24 (Spring 1978). GS issue. Includes checklist.

BOOK SECTIONS

*Adams, Timothy Dow. "GS: 'She Will Be Me When This You See.'" *Telling Lies in Modern American Autobiography* (Chapel Hill: U North Carolina P, 1990), 17–38.

*Blankley, Elyse. "Beyond the 'Talent of Knowing': GS and the New Woman." Hoffman (1986), 196–209.

*Bridgman, Richard. "GS." *The Colloquial Style in America* (NY: Oxford U P, 1966), 165–194. Rpt as *"Things as They Are* and *Three Lives,"* Bloom.

Caramello, Charles. "GS as Exemplary Theorist." Neuman & Nadel, 1–7.

*Cooley, Thomas. "The Continuous Present: GS." *Educated Lives: The Rise of Modern Autobiography in America* (Columbus: Ohio State U P, 1976), 156–181.

Couser, G Thomas. "GS: The Making of a Prophet." *American Autobiography: The Prophetic Mode* (Amherst: U Massachusetts P, 1979), 148–163.

Dachy, Marc. "How the World Is Written." Kostelanetz, 180–186.

Dearborn, Mary V. "GS's *The Making of Americans* as an Ethnic Text." *Pocahontas's Daughters* (NY: Oxford U P, 1986), 159–188.

DeKoven, Marianne. "GS and the Modernist Canon." Neuman & Nadel, 8–20.

Dydo, Ulla E. "GS: Composition as Meditation." Neuman & Nadel, 42–60.

Ford, Hugh. "GS's Plain Editions." *Published in Paris* (NY: Macmillan, 1975), 231–252.

Frieling, Kenneth. "The Becoming of GS's *The Making of Americans.*" *The Twenties,* ed Warren French (De Land, Fla: Everett/Edwards, 1975), 157–170.

*Hawkins, Susan E. "Sneak Previews: GS's Syntax in *Tender Buttons.*" Neuman & Nadel, 119–123.

Jackson, Laura Riding. "The Word-Play of GS." Hoffman (1986), 240–260.

Katz, Leon. "Matisse, Picasso and GS." Gordon, 51–63.

*Kawin, Bruce F. "The Continuous Present," "S and Beckett: Beginning Again." *Telling It Again and Again: Repetition in Literature and Film* (Ithaca, NY: Cornell U P, 1972), 108–162.

*Kellner, Bruce et al. "Friends and Enemies: A Biographical Dictionary." Kellner, 135–289.

Knight, Alan R. "Masterpieces, Manifestos and the Business of Living: GS Lecturing." Neuman & Nadel, 150–167.

Lodge, David. "GS." *The Modes of Modern Writting* (Ithaca, NY: Cornell U P, 1977), 144–155.

*Martin, Robert K. "*The Mother of Us All* and American History." Neuman & Nadel, 210–222.

Mossberg, Barbara Clarke. "A Rose in Context: The Daughter Construct." *Historical Studies and Literary Criticism,* ed Jerome J McGann (Madison: U Wisconsin P, 1985), 199–225.

Neuman, Shirley. "'Would a viper have stung her if she had only had one name?': *Doctor Faustus Lights the Lights*." Neuman & Nadel, 168–193.

Perloff, Marjorie. "(Im) Personating GS." Neuman & Nadel, 61–80.

Rieke, Alison. "GS: Mastering Pieces." *The Senses of Nonsense* (Iowa City: U Iowa P, 1992), 60–92.

Sayre, Henry M. "The Artist's Model: American Art and the Question of Looking Like GS." Neuman & Nadel, 21–41.

*Schmitz, Neil. "The Gaiety of GS," "The Genius of GS." *Huck and Alice* (Minneapolis: U Minnesota P, 1983), 160–240.

Schmitz. "The Difference of Her Likeness: GS's *Stanzas in Meditation*." Neuman & Nadel, 124–149.

Secor, Cynthia. "GS: The Complex Force of Her Femininity." *Women, the Arts, and the 1920s in Paris and New York*, ed Kenneth W Wheeler & Virginia Lee Lussier (New Brunswick, NJ: Transaction, 1982), 27–35.

Secor. "The Question of GS." *American Novelists Revisited*, ed Fritz Fleischmann (Boston: Hall, 1982), 299–310.

Spencer, Benjamin T. "GS: Non-Expatriate." *Literature and Ideas in America: Essays in Memory of Harry Hayden Clark*, ed Robert Falk (Athens: Ohio U P, 1975), 204–227.

Stimpson, Catharine R. "Gertrice/Altrude: S, Toklas, and the Paradox of the Happy Marriage." *Mothering the Mind*, ed Ruth Perry & Martine Watson Brownley (NY: Holmes & Meier, 1984), 122–139.

Stimpson. "GS and the Transposition of Gender." *The Poetics of Gender*, ed Nancy K Miller (NY: Columbia U P, 1986), 1–18.

Tanner, Tony. "GS and the Complete Actual Present." *The Reign of Wonder* (Cambridge: Cambridge U P, 1965), 187–204.

*Wilder, Thornton. "GS's Narration." *American Characteristics and Other Essays*, ed Donald Gallup; foreword by Isabel Wilder (NY: Harper & Row, 1979), 183–222.

Williams, William Carlos. "The Work of GS," "A 1 Pound Stein." *Selected Essays* (NY: Random House, 1954), 113–120, 162–166. Rpt Kostelanetz.

Wilson, Edmund. "GS." *Axel's Castle* (NY: Scribners, 1931), 237–256. Rpt Bloom.

ARTICLES

Aldington, Richard. "The Disciples of GS." *Poetry*, 17 (Oct 1920), 35–40.

Alkon, Paul K. "Visual Rhetoric in *The Autobiography of Alice B. Toklas.*" *Critical Inquiry*, 1 (Jun 1975), 849–881.

Allen, Mary. "GS's Sense of Oneness." *Southwest Review*, 66 (Winter 1981), 1–10.

*Anderson, Sherwood. "The Work of GS." *Little Review*, 8 (Spring 1922), 29–32. Rpt as intro to *Geography and Plays*. Rpt Hoffman (1986), Kostelanetz.

Banta, Martha. "James and S on 'Being American' and 'Having France.'" *French-American Review*, 3 (Fall 1979), 63–84.

*Breslin, James E. "GS and the Problems of Autobiography." *Georgia Review*, 33 (Winter 1979), 901–913. Rpt *Women's Autobiography*, ed Estelle C Jelinek (Bloomington: Indiana U P, 1980).

Burke, Carolyn. "GS, the Cone Sisters, and the Puzzle of Female Friendship." *Critical Inquiry*, 8 (Spring 1982), 543–564.

*Burke, Kenneth. "Engineering With Words." *Dial*, 74 (Apr 1923), 408–412. Rpt Hoffman (1986).

Cohen, Milton A. "Black Brutes and Mulatto Saints: The Racial Heirarchy of S's 'Melanctha.'" *Black American Literature Forum*, 18 (Fall 1984), 119–121.

Cohen, Paul. "GS: American Librettist." *Centennial Review*, 29 (Fall 1985), 389–399.

Cooper, David D. "GS's 'Magnificent Asparagus': Horizontal Meaning and Unmeaning in *Tender Buttons.*" *Modern Fiction Studies*, 20 (Autumn 1974), 337–349.

Dodge, Mabel. "Speculations, or Post-Impressionism in Prose." *Arts and Decorations*, 3 (Mar 1913), 172, 174. Rpt Hoffman (1986).

Dydo, Ulla E. "How to Read GS: The Manuscript of 'Stanzas in Meditation.'" *Text*, 1 (1981), 271–303.

Dydo. "*Stanzas in Meditation*: The Other Autobiography." *Chicago Review*, 35 (Winter 1985), 4–20. Rpt Kostelanetz.

Dydo. "Landscape Is Not Grammar: GS in 1928." *Raritan*, 7 (Summer 1987), 97–113.

Eagleson, Harvey. "GS: Method in Madness." *Sewanee Review*, 44 (Apr–Jun 1936), 164–177.

Evans, Oliver. "GS as Humorist." *Prairie Schooner*, 21 (Mar 1947), 97–101.

Farber, Lawren. "Fading: A Way. GS's Sources for *Three Lives.*" *Journal of Modern Literature*, 5 (Sep 1976), 463–480.

Fitz, L T. "GS and Picasso: The Language of Surfaces." *American Literature*, 45 (May 1973), 228–237.

Gallup, Donald. "The GS Collection." *Yale University Library Gazette*, 22 (Oct 1947), 22–32.

Gallup. "A Book Is a Book Is a Book." *New Colophon*, 1 (Jan 1948), 67–80.

Gallup. "Always Gtrde Stein." *Southwest Review*, 34 (Summer 1949), 254–258.

Gallup. "GS and the *Atlantic*." *Yale University Library Gazette*, 28 (Jan 1954), 109–128.

Gallup. "Du côté de chez Stein." *Book Collector*, 19 (Summer 1970), 169–184.

Gass, William H. "GS: Her Escape From Protective Language." *Accent*, 18 (Autumn 1958), 233–244. Rpt *Fiction and the Figures of Life* by Gass (NY: Knopf, 1970).

Gass. "GS, Geographer, I," "GS, Geographer, II." *New York Review of Books* (3 May 1973), 5–8; (17 May 1973), 25–29. Rpt as "Introduction to the Vintage Edition." *The Geographical History of America or The Relation of Human Nature to the Human Mind* (NY: Vintage, 1973).

Hastings, Susan. "Two of the Weird Sisters: The Eccentricities of GS and Edith Sitwell." *Tulsa Studies in Women's Literature*, 4 (Spring 1985), 101–123.

Kahane, Claire & Janice Doane. "Psychoanalysis and American Fiction: The Subversion of *Q.E.D.*" *Studies in American Fiction*, 9 (Autumn 1981), 137–157.

*Knight, Christopher J. "GS's 'Melanctha' and Radical Heterosexuality." *Studies in Short Fiction*, 25 (Summer 1988), 295–300.

Landon, Brooks. "'Not Solve It But Be in It': GS's Detective Stories and the Mystery of Creativity." *American Literature*, 53 (Nov 1981), 487–498.

Levinson, Ronald. "GS, William James, and Grammar." *American Journal of Psychology*, 54 (Jan 1941), 124–128.

Loy, Mina. "GS." *Transatlantic*, 2, no 3–4 (1924), 305–309, 427–430. Rpt Kellner.

Malone, Kemp. "Observations on *Paris France*." *Papers on Language and Literature*, 3 (Spring 1967), 159–178.

Mizejewski, Linda. "GS: The Pattern Moves, the Woman Behind Shakes It." *Women's Studies*, 13, no 1–2 (1986), 33–47.

Moore, Marianne. "The Spare American Emotion." *Dial*, 80 (Feb 1926), 153–156. Rpt Hoffman (1986).

*Parke, Catherine N. "'Simple Through Complication': GS Thinking." *American Literature*, 60 (Dec 1988), 554–574.

*Perloff, Marjorie. "Poetry as Word-System: The Art of GS." *American Poetry Review*, 8 (Sep–Oct 1979), 33–43. Rpt *The Poetics of Indeterminacy* by Perloff (Princeton, NJ: Princeton U P, 1981).

Porter, Katherine Anne. "'Everybody Is a Real One.'" *New York Herald Tribune Books* (16 Jan 1927), 1–2. Rpt *The Days Before* by Porter (NY: Harcourt, Brace, 1952). Rpt Bloom. Excerpted Hoffman (1986).

*Raab, Lawrence. "Remarks as Literature: *The Autobiography of Alice B. Toklas* by GS." *Michigan Quarterly Review*, 17 (Fall 1978), 480–493.

Saunders, Judith P. "Bipolar Conflict in S's 'Melanctha.'" *Modern Language Studies*, 15 (Spring 1985), 55–64.

Schaefer, James F, Jr. "An Examination of Language as Gesture in a Play by GS." *Literature in Performance*, 3 (Nov 1982), 1–14.

Schmitz, Neil. "GS as Post-Modernist: The Rhetoric of *Tender Buttons.*" *Journal of Modern Literature*, 3 (Jul 1974), 1203–1218. Rpt Hoffman (1986).

Schmitz. "Portrait, Patriarchy, Mythos: The Revenge of GS." *Salmagundi*, no 40 (Winter 1978), 69–91.

*Schwartz, Stanley. "The Autobiography as Generic 'Continuous Present': *Paris France* and *Wars I Have Seen.*" *English Studies in Canada*, 4 (Summer 1979), 224–237.

Skinner, B F. "Has GS a Secret?" *Atlantic*, 153 (Jan 1934), 50–57. Excerpted Hoffman (1986).

Steiner, Wendy. "The Steinian Portrait." *Yale University Library Gazette*, 50 (Jul 1975), 30–40.

*Stewart, Allegra. "The Quality of GS's Creativity." *American Literature*, 28 (Jan 1957), 488–506. Rpt Bloom. Excerpted Hoffman (1986).

Stimpson, Catharine R. "The Mind, the Body, and GS." *Critical Inquiry*, 3 (Spring 1977), 489–506. Rpt Bloom.

*Van Vechten, Carl. "How to Read GS." *Trend*, 7 (Aug 1914), 553–557. Excerpted Hoffman (1986).

Wight, Doris T. "Hidden Feminism in GS's Roses and Rooms." *Creative Woman*, 8 (Spring–Summer 1987), 5–9.

Wilson, Edmund. "A Guide to GS." *Vanity Fair*, 32 (Sep 1923), 60, 80.

Winston, Elizabeth. "Making History in *The Mother of Us All.*" *Mosaic*, 20 (Fall 1987), 117–129.

— *Maureen R. Liston & Gina D. Peterman*
This entry has been revised and updated by the series editors.

ANNE TYLER
Minneapolis, Minn, 25 Oct 1941–

Anne Tyler has enjoyed the praise of general readers and book reviewers for the twelve novels she has produced since 1964; but it was not until *Breathing Lessons* won the Pulitzer Prize for Fiction in 1989 that she came to be accorded the serious scholarly attention traditionally reserved for writers of the first rank. Tyler is now regarded as the creator of well-structured, sensitive novels that delineate the tragicomedy of modern life, particularly the difficulties of forging a personal identity and of maintaining clear communication between loved ones. Unusual for a late twentieth-century novelist, Tyler rarely engages in technical or stylistic experimentation; moreover, she carefully avoids most political issues in her fiction. Best known for her novels, Tyler has also produced notable short stories and book reviews.

Bibliographies

*Gardiner, Elaine & Catherine Rainwater. "A Bibliography of Writings by AT." *Contemporary American Women Writers: Narrative Strategies,* ed Rainwater & William J Scheick (Lexington: U P Kentucky, 1985), 142–152. Primary.

*Nesanovich, Stella. "An AT Checklist, 1959–1980." *Bulletin of Bibliography,* 38 (Apr–Jun 1981), 53–64. Primary & secondary.

Books

If Morning Ever Comes. NY: Knopf, 1964. Novel.

The Tin Can Tree. NY: Knopf, 1965. Novel.

A Slipping-Down Life. NY: Knopf, 1970. Novel.

The Clock Winder. NY: Knopf, 1972. Novel.

Celestial Navigation. NY: Knopf, 1974. Novel.

Searching for Caleb. NY: Knopf, 1976. Novel.
Earthly Possessions. NY: Knopf, 1977. Novel.
Morgan's Passing. NY: Knopf, 1980. Novel.
Dinner at the Homesick Restaurant. NY: Knopf, 1982. Novel.
The Accidental Tourist. NY: Knopf, 1985. Novel.
Breathing Lessons. NY: Knopf, 1988. Novel.
Saint Maybe. NY: Knopf, 1991. Novel.

Other

"'Because I Want More Than One Life.'" *Washington Post* (15 Aug 1976), Sect G, pp 1, 7. Rpt Petry, *Critical Essays on AT.* Essay.
"Still Just Writing." *The Writer on Her Work,* ed Janet Sternburg (NY: Norton, 1980), 3–16. Essay.
The Best American Short Stories, 1983, ed AT & Shannon Ravenel. Boston: Houghton Mifflin, 1983.

Manuscripts & Archives

Duke U Library, Durham, NC.

Interviews

BOOK SECTION

English, Sarah. "AT." *Dictionary of Literary Biography Yearbook: 1982* (Detroit: Bruccoli Clark/Gale, 1983), 193–194.

ARTICLES

Brown, Laurie L. "Interviews With Seven Contemporary Writers." *Southern Quarterly,* 21 (Summer 1983), 3–22.
Cook, Bruce. "New Faces in Faulkner Country." *Saturday Review,* 3 (4 Sep 1976), 39–41. Rpt Petry, *Critical Essays on AT.*

Cook. "A Writer—During School Hours." *Detroit News* (6 Apr 1980), Sect E, pp 1, 3. Rpt Petry, *Critical Essays on AT.*

*Lamb, Wendy. "An Interview With AT." *Iowa Journal of Literary Studies,* 3 (1981), 59–64. Rpt Petry, *Critical Essays on AT.*

Lueloff, Jorie. "Authoress Explains Why Women Dominate in South." *Baton Rouge Morning Advocate* (8 Feb 1965), Sect A, p 11. Rpt Petry, *Critical Essays on AT.*

*Michaels, Marguerite. "AT, Writer 8:05 to 3:30." *New York Times Book Review* (8 May 1977), 13, 42–43. Rpt Petry, *Critical Essays on AT.*

*"Olives Out of a Bottle." *Archive* [Duke U], 87 (Spring 1975), 70–79. Rpt Petry, *Critical Essays on AT.*

*Ridley, Clifford A. "AT: A Sense of Reticence Balanced by 'Oh, Well, Why Not?'" *National Observer,* 11 (22 Jul 1972), 23. Rpt Petry, *Critical Essays on AT.*

Critical Studies

BOOKS

*Petry, Alice Hall. *Understanding AT.* Columbia: U South Carolina P, 1990.

Voelker, Joseph C. *Art and the Accidental in AT.* Columbia: U Missouri P, 1989.

COLLECTIONS OF ESSAYS

*Petry, Alice Hall, ed. *Critical Essays on AT.* NY: Hall, 1992.

*Stephens, C Ralph, ed. *The Fiction of AT.* Jackson: U P Mississippi, 1990.

BOOK SECTIONS

*Carroll, Virginia Schaefer. "The Nature of Kinship in the Novels of AT." Stephens, 16–27.

Carson, Barbara Harrell. "Art's Internal Necessity: AT's *Celestial Navigation.*" Stephens, 47–54.

Evans, Elizabeth. "'Mere Reviews': AT as Book Reviewer." Petry, *Critical Essays on AT,* 233–242.

Farrell, Grace. "Killing off the Mother: Failed Matricide in *Celestial Navigation*." Petry, *Critical Essays on AT,* 221–232.

*Gilbert, Susan. "AT." *Southern Women Writers: The New Generation,* ed Tonette Bond Inge (Tuscaloosa: U Alabama P, 1990), 251–278.

Gilbert. "Private Lives and Public Issues: AT's Prize-winning Novels." Stephens, 136–145.

Gullette, Margaret Morganroth. "AT: The Tears (and Joys) Are in the Things." *Safe at Last in the Middle Years: The Invention of the Midlife Progress Novel* (Berkeley: U California P, 1988), 105–119. Rpt Stephens.

Inman, Sue Lile. "The Effects of the Artistic Process: A Study of Three Artist Figures in AT's Fiction." Stephens, 55–63.

Kanoza, Theresa. "Mentors and Maternal Role Models: The Healthy Mean Between Extremes in AT's Fiction." Stephens, 28–39.

Manning, Carol S. "Welty, T, and Traveling Salesmen: The Wandering Hero Unhorsed." Stephens, 110–118.

Marovitz, Sanford E. "AT's Emersonian Balance." Petry, *Critical Essays on AT,* 207–220.

*Robertson, Mary F. "AT: Medusa Points & Contact Points." *Contemporary American Women Writers: Narrative Strategies,* ed Catherine Rainwater & William J Scheick (Lexington: U P Kentucky, 1985), 119–142. Rpt Petry, *Critical Essays on AT.*

Wagner, Joseph B. "Beck Tull: 'The absent presence' in *Dinner at the Homesick Restaurant.*" Stephens, 73–83.

Zahlan, Anne Ricketson. "Traveling Towards the Self: The Psychic Drama of AT's *The Accidental Tourist.*" Stephens, 84–96.

ARTICLES

Betts, Doris. "The Fiction of AT." *Southern Quarterly,* 21 (Summer 1983), 23–37. Rpt *Women Writers of the Contemporary South,* ed Peggy Whitman Prenshaw (Jackson: U P Mississippi, 1984).

Bond, Adrienne. "From Addie Bundren to Pearl Tull: The Secularization of the South." *Southern Quarterly,* 24 (Spring 1986), 64–73.

Bowers, Bradley R. "AT's Insiders." *Mississippi Quarterly,* 42 (Winter 1988–1989), 47–56.

Carson, Barbara Harrell. "Complicate, Complicate: AT's Moral Imperative." *Southern Quarterly,* 31 (Fall 1992), 24–34.

Eckard, Paula Gallant. "Family and Community in AT's *Dinner at the Homesick Restaurant.*" *Southern Literary Journal,* 22 (Spring 1990), 33–44.

*Gibson, Mary Ellis. "Family as Fate: The Novels of AT." *Southern Literary Journal,* 16 (Fall 1983), 47–58. Rpt Petry, *Critical Essays on AT.*

*Jones, Anne G. "Home at Last, and Homesick Again: The Ten Novels of AT." *Hollins Critic,* 23 (Apr 1986), 1–14.

Koppel, Gene. "Maggie Moran, AT's Madcap Heroine: A Game-Approach to *Breathing Lessons.*" *Essays in Literature,* 18 (Fall 1991), 276–287.

Nesanovich, Stella. "The Individual in the Family: AT's *Searching for Caleb* and *Earthly Possessions.*" *Southern Review,* 14 (Jan 1978), 170–176. Rpt Petry, *Critical Essays on AT.*

Petry, Alice Hall. "Bright Books of Life: The Black Norm in AT's Novels." *Southern Quarterly,* 31 (Fall 1992), 7–13.

Shafer, Aileen Chris. "AT's 'The Geologist's Maid': 'Till Human Voices Wake Us and We Drown.'" *Studies in Short Fiction,* 27 (Winter 1990), 65–71.

Shelton, Frank W. "The Necessary Balance: Distance and Sympathy in the Novels of AT." *Southern Review,* 20 (Autumn 1984), 851–860. Rpt Petry, *Critical Essays on AT.*

Town, Caren J. "Rewriting the Family During *Dinner at the Homesick Restaurant.*" *Southern Quarterly,* 31 (Fall 1992), 14–23.

— *Alice Hall Petry*

EUDORA WELTY

Jackson, Miss, 13 Apr 1909–

When *A Curtain of Green*, her first collection of short stories, appeared in 1941, Eudora Welty established a writing career that would win her O. Henry Awards in 1942, 1943, and 1969 and a Pulitzer Prize for *The Optimist's Daughter* in 1972. Although the focus of her life and work is the American South, her reputation is international. She is recognized for her humor, for her use of regional speech, and for her depiction of rural people in conflict with the demands of an increasingly urban society. Many of the critical studies demonstrate how Welty uses myth, ritual, and the sense of family to find meaning in a world where people are being torn away from the land.

Bibliographies & Catalogue

Marrs, Suzanne. *The W Collection: A Guide to the EW Manuscripts and Documents at the Mississippi Department of Archives and History.* Jackson: U P Mississippi, 1988.

*McDonald, W U, Jr. "EW." *Contemporary Authors Bibliographical Series: American Novelists,* ed James J Martine (Detroit: Bruccoli Clark/Gale, 1986), 383–420. Primary & secondary; includes essay on secondary sources.

*McHaney, Pearl Amelia. "A EW Checklist: 1973–1986." *Mississippi Quarterly,* 39 (Fall 1986), 651–697. Primary & secondary.

*Thompson, Victor H. *EW: A Reference Guide.* Boston: Hall, 1976. Secondary.

Books

A Curtain of Green. Garden City, NY: Doubleday, Doran, 1941. Stories.

The Robber Bridegroom. Garden City, NY: Doubleday, Doran, 1942. Novel.

The Wide Net and Other Stories. NY: Harcourt, Brace, 1943.

Delta Wedding. NY: Harcourt, Brace, 1946. Novel.

The Golden Apples. NY: Harcourt, Brace, 1949. Stories.

Short Stories. NY: Harcourt, Brace, 1950. Rev as "Looking at Short Stories," *The Eye of the Story.* Essay.

The Ponder Heart. NY: Harcourt, Brace, 1954. Novel.

The Bride of the Innisfallen and Other Stories. NY: Harcourt, Brace, 1955.

Place in Fiction. NY: House of Books, 1957. Rpt *The Eye of the Story.* Essay.

Three Papers on Fiction. Northampton, Mass: Smith C, 1962. Essays.

The Shoebird. NY: Harcourt, Brace & World, 1964. Children's book.

A Sweet Devouring. NY: Albondocani, 1969. Rpt *The Eye of the Story.* Essay.

Losing Battles. NY: Random House, 1970. Novel.

One Time, One Place: Mississippi in the Depression, a Snapshot Album. NY: Random House, 1971. Essay & photographs.

The Optimist's Daughter. NY: Random House, 1972. Novel.

A Pageant of Birds. NY: Albondocani, 1974. Rpt *The Eye of the Story.* Essay.

Fairy Tale of the Natchez Trace. Jackson: Mississippi Historical Society, 1975. Rpt *The Eye of the Story.* Speech.

The Eye of the Story: Selected Essays and Reviews. NY: Random House, 1978.

Ida M'Toy. Urbana & c: U Illinois P, 1979. Essay & photographs.

Women!! Make Turban in Own Home! Winston-Salem, NC: Palaemon, 1979. Essay.

Acrobats in a Park. Northridge, Calif: Lord John, 1980. Story.

Bye-Bye Brevoort, a Skit. Winston-Salem, NC: Palaemon, 1980.

Twenty Photographs. Winston-Salem, NC: Palaemon, 1980. Contains 4 new photographs.

Retreat. Winston-Salem, NC: Palaemon, 1981. Story.

One Writer's Beginnings. Cambridge, Mass & London: Harvard U P, 1984. Autobiography.

In Black and White. Northridge, Calif: Lord John, 1985. Photographs.

Photographs. Jackson & London: U P Mississippi, 1989.

Other

The Norton Book of Friendship, ed EW & Ronald A Sharp. NY & London: Norton, 1991. Anthology.

Collections

Selected Stories of EW. NY: Modern Library, 1943.

Thirteen Stories, ed with intro by Ruth M Vande Keift. NY: Harcourt, Brace & World, 1965.

The Collected Stories of EW. NY & London: Harcourt Brace Jovanovich, 1980.

Manuscripts & Archives

The Mississippi Department of Archives & History, Jackson, & the Harry Ransom Humanities Research Center, U of Texas, Austin.

Interviews

BOOK

Prenshaw, Peggy Whitman, ed. *Conversations With EW.* Jackson: U P Mississippi, 1984.

BOOK SECTIONS

Ferris, Bill. "A Visit With EW." *Images of the South: Visits With EW and Walker Evans* (Memphis, Tenn: Center for Southern Folklore, 1977), 11–26. Rpt Prenshaw (1984).

Freeman, Jean Todd. "EW." *Conversations With Writers II* (Detroit: Bruccoli Clark/Gale, 1978), 284–316. Rpt Prenshaw (1984).

Jones, John. "EW." *Mississippi Writers Talking* (Jackson: U P Mississippi, 1982), 3–35. Rpt Prenshaw (1984).

Rubin, Louis D, Jr. "Growing Up in the Deep South: A Conversation With EW, Shelby Foote, and Louis Rubin, Jr." *The American South,* ed Rubin (Baton Rouge: Louisiana State U P, 1980), 59–85.

ARTICLES

Bunting, Charles T. "The Interior World: An Interview With EW." *Southern Review,* 8 (Oct 1972), 711–735. Rpt Prenshaw (1984).

Clemons, Walter. "Meeting Miss W." *New York Times Book Review* (12 Apr 1970), 2, 46.

Gretlund, Jan Nordby. "Interview With EW." *Southern Humanities Review,* 14 (Summer 1980), 193–208. Rpt Prenshaw (1984).

Kuehl, Linda. "The Art of Fiction XLVII: EW." *Paris Review,* 14 (Fall 1972), 72–97. Rpt *Writers at Work, Fourth Series,* ed George Plimpton (NY: Viking, 1976). Rpt Prenshaw (1984).

Nostrandt, Jeanne Rolfe. "Fiction or Event: An Interview With EW." *New Orleans Review,* 7, no 1 (1980), 26–34.

Powell, Dannye Romine. "An Interview With EW." *Mississippi Review,* 20, nos 1–2 (1991), 76–82.

Tyler, Anne. "A Visit With EW." *New York Times Book Review* (2 Nov 1980), 33–34.

Van Gelder, Robert. "An Interview With Miss EW." *New York Times Book Review* (14 Jun 1942), 2. Rpt *Writers and Writing* by Van Gelder (NY: Scribner, 1946). Rpt Prenshaw (1984).

Critical Studies

B O O K S

Bryant, J A, Jr. *EW.* Minneapolis: U Minnesota P, 1968.

Devlin, Albert J. *EW's Chronicle: A Story of Mississippi Life.* Jackson: U P Mississippi, 1983.

Evans, Elizabeth. *EW.* NY: Ungar, 1981.

Gygax, Franzisk. *Serious Daring From Within: Female Narrative Strategies in EW's Novels.* Westport, Conn: Greenwood, 1990.

Isaacs, Neil D. *EW.* Austin, Tex: Steck-Vaughn, 1969.

*Kreyling, Michael P. *EW's Achievement of Order.* Baton Rouge: Lousiana State U P, 1980.

*Kreyling. *Author and Agent: EW and Diarmuid Russell.* NY: Farrar, Straus & Giroux, 1991.

Manning, Carol S. *With Ears Opening Like Morning Glories: EW and the Love of Storytelling.* Westport, Conn: Greenwood, 1985.

Randisi, Jennifer Lynn. *A Tissue of Lies: EW and Southern Romance.* Washington: U P America, 1982.

*Schmidt, Peter. *The Heart of the Story: EW's Short Fiction.* Jackson: U P Mississippi, 1991.

*Vande Kieft, Ruth M. *EW.* Boston: Twayne, 1962. Rev 1987.

Westling, Louise. *Sacred Groves and Ravaged Gardens: The Fiction of EW, Carson McCullers, and Flannery O'Connor.* Athens: U Georgia P, 1985.

Westling. *EW.* Totowa, NJ: Barnes & Noble, 1989.

C O L L E C T I O N S   O F   E S S A Y S

Bloom, Harold, ed. *EW.* NY: Chelsea House, 1986.

Desmond, John F. ed *A Still Moment: Essays on the Art of EW*. Metuchen, NJ: Scarecrow, 1978.

Dollarhide, Louis & Ann J Abadie, eds. *EW: A Form of Thanks*. Jackson: U P Mississippi, 1979.

*Prenshaw, Peggy W, ed. *EW: Critical Essays*. Jackson: U P Mississippi, 1979.

Trouard, Dawn, ed. *EW: Eye of the Storyteller*. Kent, Ohio: Kent State U P, 1990.

*Turner, W Craig & Lee Emling Harding, eds. *Critical Essays on EW*. Boston: Hall, 1989.

SPECIAL JOURNALS

Eudora Welty Newsletter (semiannually, 1977-). Summer issue includes EW checklist.

Mississippi Quarterly, 26 (Fall 1973). EW issue.

Mississippi Quarterly, 39 (Fall 1986). EW issue. Rpt as *W: A Life in Literature*, ed Albert J Devlin (Jackson: U P Mississippi, 1987).

Shenandoah, 20 (Spring 1969). EW issue.

Southern Quarterly, 20 (Summer 1982). EW issue.

BOOK SECTIONS

Arnold, Marilyn. "The Strategy of Edna Earle Ponder." Trouard, 69–77.

Binding, Paul. "Mississippi and EW." *Separate Country: A Literary Journal Through the American South* (NY: Paddington, 1979), 131–148.

Brooks, Cleanth. "American Literature: Mirror, Lens or Prism?" *A Shaping Joy* (NY: Harcourt Brace Jovanovich, 1971), 166–180.

Cooley, John R. "EW." *Savages and Naturals: Black Portraits by White Writers in Modern American Literature* (Newark: U Delaware P, 1982), 124–137.

*Eisinger, Chester E. "EW and the Triumph of the Imagination." *Fiction of the Forties* (Chicago: U Chicago P, 1963), 258–283.

Evans, Elizabeth. "EW and the Dutiful Daughter." Trouard, 57–68.

Glenn, Eunice. "Fantasy in the Fiction of EW." *Critiques and Essays on Modern Fiction*, ed John W Aldridge (NY: Ronald, 1952), 506–517.

Gossett, Louise Y. "Violence as Revelation: EW." *Violence in Recent Southern Fiction* (Durham, NC: Duke U P, 1965), 98–117.

Graulich, Melody. "Pioneering the Imagination: EW's *The Robber Bridegroom*." *Women and Western American Literature*, ed Helen Winter Stauffer & Susan J Rosowski (Troy, NY: Whitston, 1982), 283–296.

*Gross, Seymour L. "EW's Comic Imagination." *The Comic Imagination in American Literature,* ed Louis D Rubin, Jr (New Brunswick, NJ: Rutgers U P, 1973), 319–328.

Holder, Alan. "'It Happened in Extraordinary Times': EW's Historical Fiction." *The Imagined Past* (Lewisburg, Pa: Bucknell U P, 1980), 125–146.

*Marrs, Suzanne. "EW's Photography: Images into Fiction." Turner & Harding, 280–296.

Pitavy-Souques, Daniele. "Of Suffering and Joy: Aspects of Storytelling in W's Short Fiction." Trouard, 142–150.

*Porter, Katherine Anne. "Introduction." *A Curtain of Green,* xi–xxiii. Rpt Bloom.

Rubin, Louis D, Jr. "The Golden Apples of the Sun." *The Faraway Country* (Seattle: U Washington P, 1963), 131–154.

ARTICLES

*Arnold, Marilyn. "Images of Memory in EW's *The Optimist's Daughter.*" *Southern Literary Journal,* 14 (Spring 1982), 28–38. Rpt Turner & Harding.

Balliett, Whitney. "Jazz: Fats." *New Yorker,* 54 (10 Apr 1978), 110–112, 114–117.

Bradford, M E. "Miss Eudora's Picture Book." *Mississippi Quarterly,* 26 (Fall 1973), 659–662.

Brinkmeyer, Robert H, Jr. "An Openness to Others: The Imaginative Vision of EW." *Southern Literary Journal,* 20 (Spring 1988), 69–80.

Brookhart, Mary Hughes & Suzanne Marrs. "More Notes on River Country." *Mississippi Quarterly,* 39 (Fall 1986), 507–519.

*Brooks, Cleanth. "The Past Reexamined: *The Optimist's Daughter.*" *Mississippi Quarterly,* 26 (Fall 1973), 577–587.

Brown, Ashley. "EW and the Mythos of Summer." *Shenandoah,* 20 (Spring 1969), 29–35.

Bryant, J A. "Seeing Double in *The Golden Apples.*" *Sewanee Review,* 82 (Spring 1974), 300–315. Rpt Turner & Harding.

Bukoski, Anthony. "Fact of Domesticity in EW's Fiction." *Southern Studies,* 24 (Fall 1985), 326–342.

Byrne, Bev. "A Return to the Source: EW's *The Robber Bridegroom* and *The Optimist's Daughter.*" *Southern Quarterly,* 24 (Spring 1986), 74–85. Rpt Turner & Harding.

Carson, Barbara Harrell. "EW's Dance With Darkness: *The Robber Bridegroom.*" *Southern Literary Journal,* 20 (Spring 1988), 51–68.

Carson, Gary. "Versions of the Artist in *A Curtain of Green:* The Unifying Imagination in EW's Early Fiction." *Studies in Short Fiction,* 15 (Fall 1978), 421–428.

Chaffee, Patricia. "Houses in the Short Fiction of EW." *Studies in Short Fiction,* 15 (Winter 1978), 112–114.

*Devlin, Albert. "EW's Historicism: Method and Vision." *Mississippi Quarterly,* 30 (Spring 1977), 213–234.

Drake, Robert Y. "The Reasons of the Heart." *Georgia Review,* 11 (Winter 1957), 420–426.

Evans, Elizabeth. "EW: The Metaphor of Music." *Southern Quarterly,* 20 (Summer 1982), 92–100.

Fabricant, Dan. "Onions and Hyacinths: Unwrapping the Fairchilds in *Delta Wedding.*" *Southern Literary Journal,* 18 (Fall 1985), 50–60.

Goudie, Andrea. "EW's Circe: A Goddess Who Strove With Men." *Studies in Short Fiction,* 13 (Fall 1976), 481–489.

*Griffith, Benjamin W. "'Powerhouse' as a Showcase of EW's Methods and Themes." *Mississippi Quarterly,* 19 (Spring 1966), 79–84.

*Hardy, John Edward. "*Delta Wedding* as Region and Symbol." *Sewanee Review,* 60 (Jul–Sep 1952), 397–417. Rpt Bloom; Turner & Harding.

Hardy. "The Achievement of EW." *Southern Humanities Review,* 2 (Summer 1968), 269–278.

Harris, A Leslie. "The Mystic Vision in *The Optimist's Daughter.*" *Studies in the Humanities,* 13 (Jun 1986), 31–41.

Hicks, Granville. "EW." *College English,* 14 (Nov 1952), 69–76. Rpt Turner & Harding.

*Holland, Robert B. "Dialogue as a Reflection of Place in *The Ponder Heart.*" *American Literature,* 35 (Nov 1963), 352–358. Rpt Turner & Harding.

Howell, Elmo. "EW and the City of Man." *Georgia Review,* 33 (Winter 1979), 770–782. Rpt Turner & Harding.

*Idol, John L, Jr. "Edna Earle Ponder's Good Country People." *Southern Quarterly,* 20 (Spring 1982), 66–75.

Jones, William M. "EW's Use of Myth in 'Death of a Traveling Salesman.'" *Journal of American Folklore,* 73 (Jan–Mar 1960), 18–23.

*Kreyling, Michael. "Myth and History: The Foes of *Losing Battles.*" *Mississippi Quarterly,* 26 (Fall 1973), 639–649. Rpt Turner & Harding.

Kreyling. "Life With People: Virginia Woolf, EW and *The Optimist's Daughter.*" *Southern Review,* 13 (Apr 1977), 250–271.

Kreyling. "Modernism in W's *A Curtain of Green*." *Southern Quarterly*, 20 (Summer 1982), 40–53. Rpt Turner & Harding.

Liscio, Lorraine. "The Female Voice of Poetry in 'The Bride of the Innisfallen.'" *Studies in Short Fiction*, 21 (Fall 1984), 357–362.

MacKethan, Lucinda H. "To See Things in Their Time: The Act of Focusing in EW's Fiction." *American Literature*, 50 (May 1978), 258–275. Rpt *The Dream of Arcady: Place and Time in Southern Literature*, ed MacKethan (Baton Rouge: Louisiana State U P, 1980).

*Marrs, Suzanne. "The Metaphor of Race in EW's Fiction." *Southern Review*, 22 (Oct 1986), 697–707.

*May, Charles. "Why Sister Lives at the P.O." *Southern Humanities Review*, 12 (Summer 1978), 243–249.

McAlpin, Sara. "Family in EW's Fiction." *Southern Review*, 18 (Jul 1982), 480–494.

Messerli, Douglas. "The Problem of Time in W's *Delta Wedding*." *Studies in American Fiction*, 5 (Autumn 1977), 227–240.

Moore, Carol A. "The Insulation of Illusion and *Losing Battles*." *Mississippi Quarterly*, 26 (Fall 1973), 651–658.

*Morris, Harry C. "EW's Use of Mythology." *Shenandoah*, 6 (Spring 1955), 34–40.

*Oates, Joyce Carol. "The Art of EW." *Shenandoah*, 20 (Spring 1969), 54–57. Rpt Bloom.

Oates. "Eudora's Web." *Atlantic*, 225 (Apr 1970), 118–120, 122.

Phillips, Robert L. "Patterns of Vision in W's *The Optimist's Daughter*." *Southern Literary Journal*, 14 (Fall 1981), 10–23.

Prenshaw, Peggy. "Persephone in EW's 'Livvie.'" *Studies in Short Fiction*, 17 (Spring 1980), 149–155.

*Price, Reynolds. "The Onlooker Smiling: An Early Reading of *The Optimist's Daughter*." *Shenandoah*, 20 (Spring 1969), 58–73. Rpt Bloom; Turner & Harding.

*Randisi, Jennifer L. "EW and the Fairy Tale." *Southern Literary Journal*, 23 (Fall 1990), 30–44.

Read, Martha. "EW." *Prairie Schooner*, 18 (Mar 1944), 74–76.

Rubin, Louis D, Jr. "Art and Artistry in Morgana, Mississippi." *Mississippi Review*, 4 (Summer 1981), 101–116. Rpt *A Gallery of Southerners* by Rubin (Baton Rouge: Louisiana State U P, 1982).

Seaman, Gerda & Ellen L Walker. "'It's All in a Way of Speaking': A Discussion of *The Ponder Heart*." *Southern Literary Journal*, 23 (Spring 1991), 65–76.

Slethaug, Gordon E. "Initiation in EW's *The Robber Bridegroom.*" *Southern Humanities Review,* 7 (Winter 1973), 77–87.

Snyder, Lynn. "Rhetoric in *The Ponder Heart.*" *Southern Literary Journal,* 21 (Spring 1989), 17–26.

Stroup, Sheila. "'We're All Part of It Together': EW's Hopeful Vision in *Losing Battles.*" *Southern Literary Journal,* 15 (Spring 1983), 42–58.

Thompson, Victor H. "The Natchez Trace in EW's 'A Still Moment.'" *Southern Literary Journal,* 6 (Fall 1973), 59–69.

*Vande Kieft, Ruth M. "The Mysteries of EW." *Georgia Review,* 15 (Fall 1961), 343–357. Rpt Bloom.

*Vande Kieft. "The Vision of EW." *Mississippi Quarterly,* 26 (Fall 1973), 517–542.

*Vande Kieft. "EW: The Question of Meaning." *Southern Quarterly,* 20 (Summer 1982), 24–39.

*Vande Kieft. "EW Visited and Revisited." *Mississippi Quarterly,* 39 (Fall 1986), 455–479.

Walter, James. "Place Dissolved in Grace: W's *Losing Battles.*" *Southern Literary Journal,* 21 (Fall 1988), 39–53.

*Warren, Robert Penn. "The Love and the Separateness in Miss W." *Kenyon Review,* 6 (Spring 1944), 246–259. Rpt *Selected Essays* by Warren (NY: Random House, 1958). Rpt Bloom; Turner & Harding.

Warren. "Under the Spell of EW." *New York Times Book Review* (2 Mar 1980), 1, 26–27.

Watkins, Floyd C. "EW's Natchez Trace in the New World." *Southern Review,* 22 (Oct 1986), 708–726.

Yaeger, Patricia S. "Because a Fire Was in My Head: EW and the Dialogic Imagination." *PMLA,* 99 (Oct 1984), 955–973. Rpt *Mississippi Quarterly,* 39 (Fall 1986), 561–586.

— *Victor H. Thompson*
This entry has been revised and updated by the series editors.

EDITH WHARTON

New York City, NY, 24 Jan 1862–St Brice-sous-Forêt, France,
11 Aug 1937

Although some of her contemporaries complained
that her works lacked warmth or were overly imitative of the novels of
Henry James, Edith Wharton was among the most widely admired American writers of fiction during the first three decades of the twentieth century.
After her death critics generally assigned her a high place within the second
rank of American writers. To some extent her work was overshadowed by
the more daring experiments in fictional form of such modernists as Ernest
Hemingway and William Faulkner; critics of the 1930s also felt uncomfort-
able with her emphasis on high society. Nevertheless, her major works, *The
House of Mirth, Ethan Frome* and *The Age of Innocence,* continued to
attract attention and earn admiration. The publication of R. W. B. Lewis's
biography in 1975 and the advent of feminist criticism stirred a revival of
interest in her life and works. Wharton is now widely recognized as one of
the two or three most important American women writers of fiction and
praised for her social analysis, satiric wit, stylistic grace, and psychological
depth.

Bibliographies

*Garrison, Stephen. *EW: A Descriptive Bibliography.* Pittsburgh, Pa: U
Pittsburgh P, 1990. Primary.

*Lauer, Kristin O & Margaret P Murray. *EW: An Annotated Secondary
Bibliography.* NY: Garland, 1990.

Books

Verses (Anon). Newport, RI: Hammett, 1878.

The Decoration of Houses, with Ogden Codman, Jr. NY: Scribners, 1897.
Nonfiction.

The Greater Inclination. NY: Scribners, 1899. Stories.

The Touchstone. NY: Scribners, 1900; *A Gift From the Grave.* London: Murray, 1900. Novel.

Crucial Instances. NY: Scribners, 1901. Stories.

The Valley of Decision, 2 vols. NY: Scribners, 1902. Novel.

Sanctuary. NY: Scribners, 1903. Novel.

The Descent of Man and Other Stories. NY: Scribners, 1904.

Italian Villas and Their Gardens. NY: Century, 1904. Nonfiction.

Italian Backgrounds. NY: Scribners, 1905. Nonfiction.

The House of Mirth. NY: Scribners, 1905. Novel.

The Fruit of the Tree. NY: Scribners, 1907. Novel.

Madame de Treymes. NY: Scribners, 1907. Novel.

The Hermit and the Wild Woman and Other Stories. NY: Scribners, 1908.

A Motor-Flight Through France. NY: Scribners, 1908. Nonfiction.

Artemis to Actaeon and Other Verse. NY: Scribners, 1909.

Tales of Men and Ghosts. NY: Scribners, 1910. Stories.

Ethan Frome. NY: Scribners, 1911. Novel.

The Reef. NY: Appleton, 1912. Novel.

The Custom of the Country. NY: Scribners, 1913. Novel.

Fighting France From Dunkerque to Belfort. NY: Scribners, 1915. Nonfiction.

Xingu and Other Stories. NY: Scribners, 1916.

Summer: A Novel. NY: Appleton, 1917.

The Marne. NY: Appleton, 1918. Novel.

French Ways and Their Meaning. NY & London: Appleton, 1919. Nonfiction.

In Morocco. NY: Scribners, 1920. Nonfiction.

The Age of Innocence. NY & London: Appleton, 1920. Novel.

The Glimpses of the Moon. NY & London: Appleton, 1922. Novel.

A Son at the Front. NY: Scribners, 1923. Novel.

Old New York: False Dawn (The 'Forties). NY & London: Appleton, 1924. Novella.

Old New York: The Old Maid (The 'Fifties). NY & London: Appleton, 1924. Novella.

Old New York: The Spark (The 'Sixties). NY & London: Appleton, 1924. Novella.

Old New York: New Year's Day (The 'Seventies). NY & London: Appleton, 1924. Novella.

The Mother's Recompense. NY & London: Appleton, 1925. Novel.

The Writing of Fiction. NY & London: Scribners, 1925. Nonfiction.

Here and Beyond. NY & London: Appleton, 1926. Stories.

Twelve Poems. London: Medici Society, 1926.

Twilight Sleep. NY & London: Appleton, 1927. Novel.

The Children. NY & London: Appleton, 1928. Repub as *The Marriage Playground.* NY: Grosset & Dunlap, 1930. Novel.

Hudson River Bracketed. NY & London: Appleton, 1929. Novel.

Certain People. NY & London: Appleton, 1930. Stories.

The Gods Arrive. NY & London: Appleton, 1932. Novel.

Human Nature. NY & London: Appleton, 1933. Stories.

A Backward Glance. NY & London: Appleton-Century, 1934. Autobiography.

The World Over. NY & London: Appleton-Century, 1936. Stories.

Ghosts. NY & London: Appleton-Century, 1937. Stories.

The Buccaneers. NY & London: Appleton-Century, 1938. Unfinished novel.

The Collected Short Stories of EW, 2 vols, ed with intro by R W B Lewis. NY: Scribners, 1968.

Fast and Loose, a Novelette (as by David Olivieri), ed with intro by Viola Hopkins Winner. Charlottesville: U P Virginia, 1977.

The House of Mirth: The Play of the Novel, with Clyde Fitch; ed with intro by Glenn Loney. Rutherford, NJ & c: Fairleigh Dickinson U P / London & Toronto: Associated U Presses, 1981.

Fast and Loose and The Buccaneers, ed Viola Hopkins Winner. Charlottesville & London: U P Virginia, 1993.

The Buccaneers, completed by Marion Mainwaring. NY: Viking, 1993.

Letters

The Letters of EW, ed with intro by R W B & Nancy Lewis. NY: Scribners, 1988.

Other

The Joy of Living by Hermann Sudermann; trans EW. NY: Scribners, 1902. Play.

The Book of the Homeless, ed EW. NY: Scribners, 1916. Miscellany.

Eternal Passion in English Poetry, ed EW & Robert Norton, with Gaillard Lapsley; preface by EW. NY & London: Appleton-Century, 1939. Poetry.

Edition & Collections

An EW Treasury, ed with intro by Arthur Hobson Quinn. NY: Appleton-Century-Crofts, 1950.

The Best Short Stories of EW, ed with intro by Wayne Andrews. NY: Scribners, 1958.

The EW Reader, ed with intro by Louis Auchincloss. NY: Scribners, 1965.

EW's Ethan Frome: The Story With Sources and Commentary, ed Blake Nevius. NY: Scribners, 1968.

The EW Omnibus, ed Gore Vidal. NY: Scribners, 1978.

Manuscripts & Archives

The major collections are at the Beinecke Library, Yale U; Princeton U Library; the Houghton Library, Harvard U; the Lilly Library, Indiana U; & the Harry Ransom Humanities Research Center, U of Texas, Austin.

Biographies

BOOKS

*Auchincloss, Louis. *EW: A Woman in Her Time.* NY: Viking, 1971.

*Lewis, R W B. *EW: A Biography.* NY: Harper & Row, 1975.

Lubbock, Percy. *Portrait of EW.* NY: Appleton-Century, 1947.

Critical Studies

BOOKS

Ammons, Elizabeth. *EW's Argument With America.* Athens: U Georgia P, 1980.

*Auchincloss, Louis. *EW.* Minneapolis: U Minnesota P, 1961.

Bell, Millicent. *EW and Henry James: The Story of Their Friendship.* NY: Braziller, 1965.

Fryer, Judith. *Felicitous Space: The Imaginative Structures of EW and Willa Cather.* Chapel Hill: U North Carolina P, 1986.

Gimbel, Wendy. *EW: Orphancy and Survival.* NY: Praeger, 1984.

Lawson, Richard H. *EW.* NY: Ungar, 1977.

Lindberg, Gary H. *EW and the Novel of Manners.* Charlottesville: U P Virginia, 1975.

McDowell, Margaret B. *EW.* Boston: Twayne, rev 1991.

*Nevius, Blake. *EW: A Study of Her Fiction.* Berkeley: U California P, 1953.

Papke, Mary E. *Verging on the Abyss: The Social Fiction of Kate Chopin and EW.* NY: Greenwood, 1990.

Rae, Catherine M. *EW's New York Quartet.* Lanham, Md: U P America, 1984.

Wagner-Martin, Linda. *The House of Mirth: A Novel of Admonition.* Boston: Twayne, 1990.

Walton, Geoffrey. *EW: A Critical Interpretation.* Rutherford, NJ: Fairleigh Dickinson U P, 1970.

Wershoven, Carol. *The Female Intruder in the Novels of EW.* Rutherford, NJ: Fairleigh Dickinson U P, 1982.

White, Barbara A. *EW: A Study of the Short Fiction.* NY: Twayne, 1991.

*Wolff, Cynthia Griffin. *A Feast of Words: The Triumph of EW.* NY: Oxford U P, 1977.

COLLECTIONS OF ESSAYS

*Bendixen, Alfred & Annette Zilversmit, eds. *EW: New Critical Essays.* NY: Garland, 1992.

*Bloom, Harold, ed. *EW.* NY: Chelsea House, 1986.

*Howe, Irving, ed. *EW: A Collection of Critical Essays.* Englewood Cliffs, NJ: Prentice-Hall, 1962.

SPECIAL JOURNALS

College Literature, 14 (Fall 1987). EW issue.

Edith Wharton Newsletter, (semiannually, 1984–).

Library Chronicle of the University of Texas, ns 31 (1985). EW issue.

BOOK SECTIONS

Brown, E K. "*EW.*" *The Art of the Novel,* ed Pelham Edgar (NY: Macmillan, 1933), 196–205. Rpt Howe.

Jessup, Josephine Lurie. "EW: Drawing-Room Devotee." *The Faith of Our Feminists: A Study in the Novels of EW, Ellen Glasgow, Willa Cather* (NY: Smith, 1950), 14–33, passim.

Poirier, Richard. "EW: *The House of Mirth.*" *The American Novel From James Fenimore Cooper to William Faulkner,* ed Wallace Stegner (NY: Basic Books, 1965), 117–132. Excerpted *A World Elsewhere* by Poirier (NY: Oxford U P, 1966).

Tintner, Adeline R. "Mothers, Daughters, and Incest in the Late Novels of EW." *The Lost Tradition: Mothers and Daughters in Literature,* ed Cathy N Davidson & E M Broner (NY: Ungar, 1980), 147–156.

*Tuttleton, James W. "EW: Social Historian of Old New York." *The Novel of Manners in America* (Chapel Hill: U North Carolina P, 1972), 122–140.

ARTICLES

Ammons, Elizabeth. "New Literary History: EW and Jessie Redmon Fauset." *College Literature,* 14 (Fall 1987), 207–218.

*Bernard, Kenneth. "Imagery and Symbolism in *Ethan Frome.*" *College English,* 23 (Dec 1961), 178–184. Rpt *EW's Ethan Frome: The Story With Sources and Commentary.*

Blackall, Jean Frantz. "EW's Art of Ellipsis." *Journal of Narrative Technique,* 17 (Spring 1987), 145–162.

Bloom, Lillian D. "On Daring to Look Back With W and Cather." *Novel,* 10 (Winter 1977), 167–178.

Blum, Virginia L. "EW's Erotic Other World." *Literature and Psychology,* 33, no 1 (1987), 12–29.

*Brennan, Joseph X. "*Ethan Frome:* Structure and Metaphor." *Modern Fiction Studies,* 7 (Winter 1961–1962), 347–356.

Buitenhuis, Peter. "EW and the First World War." *American Quarterly,* 18 (Fall 1966), 493–505.

Candido, Joseph. "EW's Final Alterations of *The Age of Innocence.*" *Studies in American Fiction,* 6 (Spring 1978), 21–31.

Coard, Robert L. "EW's Influence on Sinclair Lewis." *Modern Fiction Studies,* 31 (Autumn 1985), 511–527.

Cohn, Jan. "The Houses of Fiction: Domestic Architecture in Howells and EW." *Texas Studies in Literature and Language,* 15 (Fall 1973), 537–549.

Coxe, Louis O. "What EW Saw in Innocence." *New Republic,* 132 (27 Jun 1955), 16–18. Rpt Howe.

Crowley, John W. "The Unmastered Streak: Feminist Themes in W's *Summer.*" *American Literary Realism,* 15 (Spring 1982), 86–96.

*Dahl, Curtis. "EW's *The House of Mirth:* Sermon on a Text." *Modern Fiction Studies,* 21 (Winter 1975–1976), 572–576.

*Dimock, Wai-chee. "Debasing Exchange: EW's *The House of Mirth.*" *PMLA,* 100 (Oct 1985), 783–792. Rpt Bloom.

Dixon, Roslyn. "Reflecting Vision in *The House of Mirth.*" *Twentieth Century Literature,* 33 (Spring 1987), 211–222.

Dupree, Ellen Phillips. "W, Lewis and the Nobel Prize Address." *American Literature,* 56 (May 1984), 262–270.

Eggenschwiler, David. "The Ordered Disorder of *Ethan Frome.*" *Studies in the Novel,* 9 (Fall 1977), 237–246.

Fetterley, Judith. "'The Temptation to Be a Beautiful Object.'" *Studies in American Fiction,* 5 (Autumn 1977), 199–211.

Friedman, Henry J. "The Masochistic Character in the Work of EW." *Seminars in Psychiatry,* 5 (Aug 1973), 313–329.

Funston, Judith E. "'Xingu': EW's Velvet Gauntlet." *Studies in American Fiction,* 12 (Autumn 1984), 227–234.

Gargano, James W. "EW's *The Reef:* The Genteel Woman's Quest for Knowledge." *Novel,* 10 (Fall 1976), 40–48.

Gargano. "Tableaux of Renunciation: W's Use of *The Shaughran* in *The Age of Innocence.*" *Studies in American Fiction,* 15 (Spring 1987), 1–11.

Gilbert, Sandra M. "Life's Empty Pack: Notes Toward a Literary Daughteronomy." *Critical Inquiry,* 11 (Mar 1985), 355–384.

Hopkins, Viola. "The Ordering Style of *The Age of Innocence.*" *American Literature,* 30 (Nov 1958), 345–357.

Hovey, R B. "*Ethan Frome:* A Controversy About Modernizing It." *American Literary Realism,* 19 (Fall 1986), 4–20.

*Howe, Irving. "The Achievement of EW." *Encounter,* 19 (Jul 1962), 45–52. Rpt Howe.

Kaplan, Amy. "EW's Profession of Authorship." *ELH,* 53 (Summer 1986), 433–457.

Kazin, Alfred. "The Lady and the Tiger: EW and Theodore Dreiser." *Virginia Quarterly Review,* 17 (Winter 1941), 101–119. Rpt as "Two

Educations: EW and Theodore Dreiser," *On Native Grounds* by Kazin (NY: Reynal & Hitchcock, 1942). Rpt as "EW," Howe.

Kronenberger, Louis. "EW's New York: Two Period Pieces." *Michigan Quarterly Review,* 4 (Winter 1965), 3–13.

Leavis, Q D. "Henry James's Heiress: The Importance of EW." *Scrutiny,* 7 (Dec 1938), 261–276. Rpt Howe.

Lewis, R W B. "Powers of Darkness." *Times Literary Supplement* (13 Jun 1975), 644–645.

Lidoff, Joan. "Another Sleeping Beauty: Narcissism in *The House of Mirth.*" *American Quarterly,* 32 (Winter 1980), 519–539. Rpt *American Realism: New Essays,* ed Eric J Sundquist (Baltimore, Md: Johns Hopkins U P, 1982).

McDowell, Margaret B. "EW's Ghost Stories." *Criticism,* 12 (Spring 1970), 133–152.

*McDowell. "Viewing the Custom of Her Country: EW's Feminism." *Contemporary Literature,* 15 (Autumn 1974), 521–538.

McDowell. "EW's *The Old Maid:* Novella/Play/Film." *College Literature,* 14 (Fall 1987), 246–262.

*Michelson, Bruce. "EW's House Divided." *Studies in American Fiction,* 12 (Autumn 1984), 199–215.

Morante, Linda. "The Desolation of Charity Royall: Imagery in EW's *Summer.*" *Colby Library Quarterly,* 18 (Dec 1982), 241–248.

Morrow, Nancy. "Games and Conflict in EW's *The Custom of the Country.*" *American Literary Realism,* 17 (Spring 1984), 32–39.

Murphy, John J. "EW's Italian Triptych: *The Valley of Decision.*" *Xavier Review,* 4 (May 1965), 85–94.

*Murphy. "The Satiric Structure of W's *The Age of Innocence.*" *Markham Review,* 2 (May 1970), 1–4.

*Plante, Patricia R. "EW as a Short Story Writer." *Midwest Quarterly,* 4 (Jul 1963), 363–379.

Price, Alan. "The Composition of EW's *The Age of Innocence.*" *Yale University Library Gazette,* 55 (Jul 1980), 22–30.

Ransom, John Crowe. "Characters and Character: A Note on Fiction." *American Review,* 6 (Jan 1936), 271–288. Rpt *EW's Ethan Frome: The Story With Sources and Commentary.*

Rose, Alan Henry. "'Such Depths of Sad Initiation': EW and New England." *New England Quarterly,* 50 (Sep 1977), 423–439.

Saunders, Judith P. "A New Look at the Oldest Profession in W's *New Year's Day.*" *Studies in Short Fiction,* 17 (Spring 1980), 121–126.

Schriber, Mary Suzanne. "EW and Travel Writing as Self-Discovery." *American Literature*, 59 (May 1987), 257–267.

Sensibar, Judith L. "EW Reads the Bachelor Type: Her Critique of Modernism's Representative Man." *American Literature*, 60 (Dec 1988), 575–590.

*Showalter, Elaine. "The Death of the Lady (Novelist): W's *House of Mirth.*" *Representations*, 9 (Winter 1985), 133–149. Rpt Bloom.

Smith, Allan Gardner. "EW and the Ghost Story." *Women and Literature*, 1 (1980), 149–159. Rpt Bloom.

Tintner, Adeline R. "'The Hermit and the Wild Woman': EW's 'Fictioning' of Henry James." *Journal of Modern Literature*, 4 (Sep 1974), 32–42.

Tintner. "Jamesian Structures in *The Age of Innocence* and Related Stories." *Twentieth Century Literature*, 26 (Fall 1980), 332–347.

Tintner. "The Narrative Structure of *Old New York:* Text and Pictures in EW's Quartet of Linked Short Stories." *Journal of Narrative Technique*, 17 (Winter 1987), 76–82.

*Trilling, Diana. "*The House of Mirth* Revisited." *Harper's Bazaar*, 81 (Dec 1947), 126–127, 181–186. Rev *American Scholar*, 32 (Winter 1962–1963), 113–128. Rpt Howe.

Vidal, Gore. "Of Writers and Class: In Praise of EW." *Atlantic*, 241 (Feb 1978), 64–77. Rpt as "Introduction," *The EW Omnibus.*

Wegelin, Christof. "EW and the Twilight of the International Novel." *Southern Review*, 5 (Apr 1969), 398–418.

White, Barbara A. "EW's *Summer* and 'Woman's Fiction.'" *Essays in Literature*, 11 (Fall 1984), 223–235.

*Wilson, Edmund. "Justice to EW." *New Republic*, 95 (29 Jun 1938), 209–213. Rpt *The Wound and the Bow* by Wilson (Boston: Houghton Mifflin, 1941). Rpt Howe.

*Wolff, Cynthia Griffin. "'Cold Ethan' and 'Hot Ethan.'" *College Literature*, 14 (Fall 1987), 230–245.

— *Alfred Bendixen*

A CHECKLIST FOR STUDENTS
OF AMERICAN FICTION

Sixty-eight works and five periodicals essential to the study of modern American fiction.

These reference sources are intended to aid research on general aspects of American literature and its connections with other fields. Tools specific to genres, periods, and authors are listed under those rubrics in the appropriate Essential Bibliography of American Fiction volumes.

Historical Background

1. *American Studies: An Annotated Bibliography,* ed Jack Salzman. Cambridge: Cambridge U P, 1986. 3 vols. Supplement, 1990.
   Summaries of books on U.S. society & culture; well-organized, useful index.
2. *Dictionary of American Biography,* ed Allen Johnson, Dumas Malone et al. NY: Scribners, 1928– . 20 vols, 8 supplements & index.
   Generally excellent scholarly essays with brief bibliographies.
3. *Dictionary of American History,* ed Louise B Katz. NY: Scribners, 1976–1978. 7 vols & index.
   Careful identification of events, places & movements. For biographies, use *DAB* (#2).
4. *Encyclopedia of American Facts and Dates* by Gorton Carruth. 8th ed, NY: Harper & Row, 1987.
   Best chronology of American history.
5. *Guide to the Study of the United States of America: Representative Books Reflecting the Development of American Life and Thought,* ed Roy P Basler et al. Washington: Library of Congress, 1960. Supplement, 1976.
   Annotated list of titles.
6. *Harvard Guide to American History,* ed Frank Freidel. Cambridge: Harvard U P, rev 1974. 2 vols.
   Selective topical bibliographies.
7. *Oxford Companion to American History,* ed Thomas H Johnson. NY: Oxford U P, 1966.

8. *Oxford History of the American People* by Samuel Eliot Morison. NY: Oxford U P, 1965.

The American Language

9. *The American Language: An Inquiry into the Development of English in the United States* by H L Mencken. 4th ed, NY: Knopf, 1936. Supplements, 1945 & 1948.
Personalized narrative on history & quirks of written & spoken American English.
10. *Dictionary of American English on Historical Principles,* ed William A Craigie & James R Hulbert. Chicago: U Chicago P, 1938–1944. 4 vols. American complement to *OED* (#12).
11. *New Dictionary of American Slang,* ed Robert L Chapman. NY: Harper & Row, 1986.
12. *Oxford English Dictionary.* 2nd ed, ed J A Simpson & E S C Weiner, Oxford: Oxford U P, 1989. 20 vols. †
A historical dictionary, chronicling meanings & usage of 500,000 words over a millennium. Heavily British, so balanced by Craigie & Hulbert (#10).

Literature

QUOTATIONS

13. *Familiar Quotations: A Collection of Passages, Phrases, and Proverbs Traced to their Sources in Ancient and Modern Literature* by John Bartlett. 16th ed, ed Justin Kaplan et al. Boston: Little, Brown, 1992.
Standard, updated compilation, arranged by author & date; well-indexed.
14. *A New Dictionary of Quotations on Historical Principles From Ancient and Modern Sources* by H L Mencken. NY: Knopf, 1942.
Among the many books of quotations, this may rank highest for literary interest.

LITERARY HISTORIES

15. *Annals of American Literature 1602–1983,* ed Richard M Ludwig & Clifford A Nault, Jr. NY: Oxford U P, 1986.
Chronology of significant literary events & publications.

† Daggers indicate works that are at least partly available by computer. See note on "Computer Availability" at the end of this checklist.

16. *Cambridge History of American Literature,* ed William Peterfield Trent et al. Cambridge: Cambridge U P/NY: Putnam, 1917–1921. 4 vols.
Exhaustive treatment for 17th through 19th centuries.
17. *Literary History of the United States: History.* 4th ed, ed Robert E Spiller et al. NY: Macmillan/London: Collier Macmillan, 1974.
Particularly strong for pre-World War I literature & background. See # 45.

LITERARY DICTIONARIES

18. *Benét's Reader's Encyclopedia of American Literature,* ed George Perkins, Barbara Perkins & Philip Leininger. NY: Harper Collins, 1991.
Lively discussion of authors, terms & historical allusions.
19. *A Handbook to Literature* by C Hugh Holman. 6th ed, NY: Macmillan, 1992.
Essential dictionary of literary terminology. Comprehensive, with useful appendixes.
20. *Oxford Companion to American Literature.* 5th ed, ed James D Hart, NY: Oxford U P, 1983.
Oxford Companions are standards of pithy identifications of authors, works, characters in literature & may also contain useful appendixes.

LITERARY BIOGRAPHIES

21. *American Women Writers: A Critical Reference Guide From Colonial Times to the Present,* ed Lina Mainiero. NY: Ungar, 1979–1982. 4 vols.
Critical biography & selected bibliography for 1,000 writers, many not covered elsewhere.
22. *American Writers.* NY: Scribners, 1974. 4 vols. 2-vol supplements, 1979, 1981, 1991.
Scholarly essays with selective bibliographies. Based on the *U Minnesota Pamphlets on American Writers.*
23. *Black American Writers, Past and Present: A Biographical and Bibliographical Dictionary,* ed Theressa Gunnels Rush et al. Metuchen, NJ: Scarecrow, 1975.
Uneven guide to 2,000 writers.
24. *Contemporary Authors: A Bio-Bibliographical Guide to Current Writers in Fiction, General NonFiction, Poetry, Journalism, Drama, Motion Pictures, Television, and Other Fields.* Detroit: Gale, 1962– . 160 vols to date.†
Biographical, occasionally critical, information, regularly revised,

very current. *Bibliographic Series*, 2 volumes to date, provides extensive bibliographies on authors.

25. *Dictionary of Literary Biography*. Detroit: Bruccoli Clark Layman/Gale, 1978– . 162 vols to date.
    Scholarly, illustrated, critical-biographical essays with bibliographies. Individual volumes cover international literatures by nationality, genre & period. Includes *Yearbook* and *Documentary Series* volumes. Also *Concise Dictionary of American Literary Biography*, 1987–1989, 6 vols. Cumulatively indexed.

26. *Twentieth Century Authors*, ed Stanley J Kunitz & Howard Haycraft. NY: Wilson, 1942. Supplement, ed Kunitz & Vineta Colby, 1955.

27. *World Authors, 1950–1970*, ed John Wakeman. NY: Wilson, 1975. Supplements, *1970–1975* (1980); *1975–1980*, ed Vineta Colby (1985); *1980–1985*, ed Colby (1991).

PRIMARY BIBLIOGRAPHIES

28. *Bibliography of American Literature*, ed Jacob Blanck. New Haven, Conn: Yale U P, 1955–1991. 9 vols.
    Primary bibliographies of books by nearly 300 authors who died before 1931.

29. *Books in Print*. NY: Bowker, 1948– . Annually with updates.†
    Listing by author, title & subject of books available from or projected by major American publishers.

30. *Cumulative Book Index*. NY: Wilson, 1933– . Quarterly, cumulated annually. †
    English-language books published internationally. See # 37.

31. *First Printings of American Authors: Contributions Toward Descriptive Checklists*. Detroit: Bruccoli Clark/Gale, 1977–1987. 5 vols.
    Listings for many authors not found elsewhere.

32. *Facts On File Bibliography of American Fiction: 1919–1988*, 2 vols, ed Matthew J Bruccoli & Judith S Baughman; *1866–1918*, 1 vol, ed James Nagel & Gwen L Nagel; *1588–1865*, 1 vol, ed Kent P Lungquist. NY: Manly/ Facts On File, 1991–1993.
    Listings of books & selected criticism of authors between 1588 and 1988.

33. *National Union Catalog, Pre-1956 Imprints*. London: Mansell, 1968–1980. 685 vols. Supplementary vols 686–754.
    Listing by author of all books published before 1956 & owned by American research libraries, including the Library of Congress. Basic bibliographical information with locations.

34. *National Union Catalog, 1956–1967*, 125 vols, Totowa, NJ: Rowman & Littlefield, 1972; *1968–1972*, 104 vols, Ann Arbor, Mich: Edwards,

1973; *1973–1977,* 135 vols, Totowa, NJ: Rowman & Littlefield, 1978. Annual, 1974– .

Continuation of # 33 in book form; since 1983 issued on microfiche. Large portion of NUC available in MARC database.

35. *New Serial Titles, 1950–70: A Union List of Serials Commencing Publication after December 31, 1949.* Washington: Library of Congress, 1973. 4 vols. Updates: *1971–75* (1976), 2 vols; *1976–80* (1981), 2 vols; *1981–85* (1986), 6 vols; *1986–89* (1990), 6 vols.

36. *Union List of Serials in Libraries of the United States and Canada.* 3rd ed, NY: Wilson, 1965. 5 vols.

Limited by age, but best listing of major libraries' holdings of journals that began before 1950.

37. *United States Catalog: Books in Print.* NY: Wilson, 1899–1928. 4 vols, 7 supplements.

Periodic cumulation from publishers' catalogues, arranged by author, title & subject. Continued by *CBI* (# 30).

38. *United States Newspaper Program National Union List.* 3rd ed, Dublin, Ohio: OCLC, 1989.

Ongoing cooperative listing of all library holdings, with locations & exact holdings, both paper & microfilm.

INDEXES TO PRIMARY SOURCES

39. *Reader's Guide to Periodical Literature: An Author and Subject Index.* NY: Wilson, 1900– . Monthly, with quarterly & annual cumulations.†

Guide to popular, nontechnical magazines.

40. *Short Story Index: An Index to Stories in Collections and Periodicals.* NY: Wilson, 1953– .

Annual, periodic cumulations.

BIBLIOGRAPHIES OF CRITICISM

41. *The American Novel 1789–1959: A Checklist of Twentieth-Century Criticism* by Donna L Gerstenberger & George Hendrick. Denver: Swallow, 1961. *Volume II: Criticism Written 1960–1968,* Chicago: Swallow, 1970.

Listing by novelist & by novel. Good starting point.

42. *American Short-Fiction Criticism and Scholarship, 1959–1977: A Checklist* by Joe Weixlmann. Chicago: Swallow, 1982.

Comprehensive, accurate & usable.

43. *Articles on Twentieth-Century Literature: An Annotated Bibliography, 1954–70,* ed David E Pownall. Millwood, NY: Kraus, 1973–1980. 7 vols.

International in scope of subjects & journals indexed.

44. *The Contemporary Novel: A Checklist of Critical Literature on the British and American Novel Since 1945* by Irving Adelman & Rita Dworkin. Metuchen, NJ: Scarecrow, 1972.
    Criticism of 200 authors, listed by novelist & novel.
45. *Literary History of the United States: Bibliography.* 4th ed, ed Robert E Spiller et al. NY: Macmillan / London: Collier Macmillan, 1974.
    Awkward but important combination of three previously published bibliographies covering pre-1948, 1948–1958, 1958–1970. See # 17.
46. *Short Fiction Criticism: A Checklist of Interpretation Since 1925 of Stories and Novelettes (American, British, Continental), 1800–1958,* ed Jarvis Thurston et al. Denver: Swallow, 1960.
    Useful for early criticism; updated by Weixlmann (# 42).
47. *Sixteen Modern American Authors: A Survey of Research and Criticism,* ed Jackson R Bryer. Durham, NC: Duke U P, rev 1974. Vol 2 (1989) covers 1972–1988.
    S Anderson, Cather, S Crane, Dreiser, Eliot, Faulkner, Fitzgerald, Frost, Hemingway, O'Neill, Pound, Robinson, Steinbeck, Stevens, W C Williams & Wolfe.
48. *Twentieth-Century Short Story Explication, 1900–1975* by Warren S Walker. 3rd ed, Hamden, Conn: Shoe String, 1977. Supplements, *1976–1978* (1980), *1977–1981* (1984), *1981–1984* (1987), *1984–1986* (1989), *1987–1988* (1991). Index (1992).
    Extensive, but difficult to use. Journal abbreviations defined in supplements.

PERIODICAL GUIDES TO CRITICISM

49. *Abstracts of English Studies.* Calgary: U Calgary P, 1958– . Quarterly.
    International guide to articles & essays, many not indexed elsewhere, on English & American literature.
50. *American Literary Scholarship.* Durham, NC: Duke U P, 1965– . Annual.
    Bibliographic essays on genres, authors, periods.
51. *Annual Bibliography of English Language and Literature.* Cambridge, UK: Modern Humanities Research Association, 1920– . Annual.
    International, arranged by topic. Supplements *MLAIB* (#57).
52. *Book Review Digest.* NY: Wilson, 1905– . 10 times per year, cumulated annually.†
    Excerpts from reviews of popular books in magazines & newspapers.
53. *Book Review Index.* Detroit: Gale, 1965– . Bi-monthly, cumulated.†
    Far more comprehensive than # 52; especially good for scholarly books & novels receiving limited attention.
54. *Combined Retrospective Index to Book Reviews in Humanities Journals, 1802–1974.* Woodbridge, Conn: Research Publications, 1982–1984. 10 vols.

500,000 reviews from 150 journals listed; especially strong in literature.

55. *Contemporary Literary Criticism: Excerpts From the Criticism of Today's Novelists, Poets, Playwrights and Other Creative Writers.* Detroit: Gale, 1973– .

International coverage, long excerpts from criticism. Format similar to *TCLC* (#58).

56. *Humanities Index.* NY: Wilson, 1974– . Quarterly, cumulated annually.†

Not as comprehensive as *MLAIB* (# 57), but interdisciplinary, covering history, philosophy, theology, as well as language & literature. Valuable for timeliness. Supersedes *International Index* (1907–1965) & *Social Sciences and Humanities Index* (1965–1974).

57. *MLA International Bibliography of Books and Articles on the Modern Languages and Literature.* NY: MLA, 1921– . Annual.†

Extensive, international coverage of American literature; since 1981 enhanced by subject index. Arrangement by nationality & period. Must be supplemented by other indexes.

58. *Twentieth-Century Literary Criticism: Excerpts From Criticism of the Works of Novelists, Poets, Playwrights, Short Story Writers, and Other Creative Writers, 1990–1960, From the First Published Critical Appraisals to Current Evaluations.* Detroit: Gale, 1978– .

GUIDES TO RESEARCH

59. *Bibliographical Guide to the Study of the Literature of the U.S.A.* by Clarence L Gohdes & Sanford E Marovitz. 5th ed, Durham, NC: Duke U P, 1984.

Annotated listing, especially good for topical approach.

60. *Literary Research Guide: A Guide to Reference Sources for the Study of Literatures in English and Related Topics* by James L Harner. NY: MLA, 1989.

Useful manual for using the library. Hundreds of annotations on selected reference books; appendixes.

BOOKS & PUBLISHING

61. *The Book in America: A History of the Making and Selling of Books in the United States* by Hellmut Lehmann-Haupt et al. 2nd ed, NY: Bowker, 1952.

62. *Glaister's Glossary of the Book* by Geoffrey Ashall Glaister. 2nd ed, London: Allen & Unwin, 1979.

Treats all aspects of the book & publishing. Illustrations & appendixes.

63. *Guide to the Study of United States Imprints* by G Thomas Tanselle. Cambridge: Harvard U P, 1971. 2 vols.

Comprehensive checklists of materials on all aspects of printing &
publishing history. See also *DLB* (#25), vol 46.
64. *A History of American Magazines* by Frank Luther Mott. Cambridge:
Harvard U P, 1938–1968. 5 vols.
Covers 1741–1930, by period, genre & specific titles.
65. *History of Book Publishing in the United States* by John W Tebbel. NY:
Bowker, 1973–1981. 4 vols.

DIRECTORIES

66. *Literary Market Place: The Directory of American Book Publishing.* NY:
Bowker, 1940– . Annual.
Addresses & information for publishers, agents, reviewers, book clubs, etc.
67. *MLA Directory of Periodicals: A Guide to Journals and Series in
Languages and Literatures.* NY: MLA, 1979– . Annual.
Listing of all serials indexed by *MLAIB* (#57).
68. *Ulrich's International Periodicals Directory.* NY: Bowker, 1932– .
Annual.†
Best listing of currently published titles by subject; valuable for listing
of indexes that cover each journal.

Important Journals

J-1. *American Literature: A Journal of Literary History, Criticism, and
Bibliography.* Durham, NC: Duke U P, 1929– . Quarterly.
Critical articles, book reviews, research in progress; formerly thor-
ough, now selective bibliography.
J-2. *American Quarterly.* Philadelphia: U Pennsylvania P, 1949– . Quar-
terly.
Explores the cultural background of literature. Bibliographical essays.
J-3. *Modern Fiction Studies.* West Lafayette, Ind: Purdue U, Department of
English, 1955– . Quarterly.
J-4. *Resources for American Literary Study.* College Park: U Maryland,
Department of English, 1971– . Semiannual.
J-5. *Studies in American Fiction.* Boston. Northeastern U, Department of
English, 1973– . Semiannual.

— *Daniel Boice*

COMPUTER AVAILABILITY

Reference works for American fiction are increasingly available through computer technology. Some are accessible on CD-ROM or on computerized catalogues of large libraries. Others are "on-line" tools, which are used via telephone linkage to computer centers or databases. More and more tools can be used in several of these formats, and reference librarians can advise on which tools are available at individual libraries.

Advantages of computerized resources include speed, ability to look for several topics at once, and printing out of citations. Factors that determine the usefulness of these tools include the reliability of both data and method, ease of use, and especially scope—that is, how broadly the tool covers the subject and what years and journals it indexes. Many computerized tools cover only recent years and must be supplemented by using printed versions.

Titles in the Checklist that are at least partially available by computer are marked by daggers †. Reference librarians will be able to provide advice and direction. Other major computer tools include:

OCLC (Online Computer Library Center): A network including nearly all American libraries and many foreign ones. Lists millions of books, journals, maps, recordings and archival materials. Especially useful for identifying libraries with specific titles.

RLIN (Research Libraries Network): Listing of items held by the leading American research libraries, the Research Libraries Group. Good for all library materials, especially archives.

Both the *OCLC* and *RLIN* databases include the recent Library of Congress cataloguing, called *MARC* (Machine Readable Cataloguing). The strength of *OCLC* is its broad coverage of libraries, but *RLIN* is more careful in its cataloguing. Both *RLIN* and *OCLC* offer several ways to locate books, beyond the traditional avenues of author and title. Librarians will provide information regarding availability of these tools.

— *Daniel Boice*

MODERN WOMEN WRITERS:
Basic Bibliographical Sources

Duke, Maurice, Jackson R Bryer & M Thomas Inge, eds. *American Women Writers: Bibliographic Essays.* Westport, Conn: Greenwood, 1983.

Inge, Tonnette Bond. *Southern Women Writers: The New Generation.* Tuscaloosa & London: U Alabama P, 1990.

Magee, Rosemary M, ed. *Friendship and Sympathy: Communities of Southern Women Writers.* Jackson & London: U P Mississippi, 1992.

Manning, Carol S, ed. *The Female Tradition in Southern Literature.* Urbana & Chicago: U Illinois P, 1993.

Showalter, Elaine, ed. *Modern American Women Writers.* NY: Scribners, 1991.

White, Barbara Anne, ed. *American Women Writers: An Annotated Bibliography of Criticism.* NY: Garland, 1977.

— Mary Ann Wimsatt